Parables Told by Jesus

Parables Told by Jesus

A Contemporary Approach to the Parables

By

Wilfrid J. Harrington, O.P.

ALBA · HOUSE   NEW · YORK

SOCIETY OF ST. PAUL, 2187 VICTORY BLVD., STATEN ISLAND, NEW YORK 10314

Acknowledgment:

The Scripture quotations in this publication are from the Revised Standard Version Bible copyright 1946, 1952, and ©1971 by the Division of Christian Education of the National Council of Churches of Christ in the U.S.A. and used by permission.

Library of Congress Cataloging in Publication Data

Harrington, Wilfred J.
  Parables told by Jesus; a contemporary approach.

  Bibliography: p.
  1. Jesus Christ—Parables.   I.   Title.
BT375.2.H33   1975   226'.8'066   74-12395
ISBN 0-8189-0296-5

Imprimi Potest:
Flannan Hynes, O.P.
Provincial

Nihil Obstat:
Benedict Hegarty, O.P.
Liam Walsh, O.P.

Nihil Obstat:
Daniel V. Flynn, J.C.D.
Censor Librorum

Imprimatur:
✠ James P. Mahoney, D.D.
Vicar General, Archdiocese of New York
June 25, 1974

*Designed, printed and bound in the United States of
America by the Fathers and Brothers of the Society of St. Paul,
2187 Victory Boulevard, Staten Island, New York, 10314,
as part of their communications apostolate.*

5 6 7 8 9 (*Current Printing: first digit*).

PREFACE

A decade ago I played some part in popularizing a new and decisive turn in the study of the parables of Jesus,[1] for it is undeniable that C. H. Dodd and Joachim Jeremias have provided insights and developed an approach to the parables which have profoundly influenced our understanding of them. The present book is intended to show how more recent studies on the parables have helped us, even further, to hear them aright. In particular, it emerges that a certain dogmatism on questions of literary form and historical setting can hamper the application of the parables and weaken their relevance. The parabolic teaching of Jesus must still be seen as rich beyond our imaginings. The richness of this treasure is only discovered, in the end, by looking straight at the parables which, as the plain "earthenware vessels" they really are (cf. 2 Cor 4:7), contain the treasure.

Jesus taught in parables. The Gospels bear abundant witness to the fact that the first Christians turned to his parables as to living words which spoke directly to themselves. Already we are assured that we, too, should hear them spoken to us. But we must begin by understanding. We must discern, if we can, the original import of a parable; we must look for any sign of adaptation or reinterpretation in the early preaching tradition; we must appreciate the purpose of an evangelist in his choice and presentation of any particular parable. For, if we are to be guided by, and live by, the words of Jesus, we must be sure that our application of his words by ourselves and to our situation is along the right lines. The professional exegete may be expected to provide some help.

I have begun by giving some indication of the tendencies of more recent work on the parables. Then I have shown how evangelists have fitted parables of Jesus into the pattern of their own theology and used them to cast light on their contemporary Christian situation. The parables may be arranged in groups—the parables of the Kingdom is an obvious grouping. It is less generally recognized that there is a homogeneous group of Servant Parables; the study of them is illuminating. Finally, after this more general treatment, I have sought to illustrate the approach of each of the synoptists by the study of a particular parable in each. It is hoped that, in this manner, both on a broader basis and in the concrete, fresh light has been brought to bear on some, at least, of the parables of Jesus.

W.J.H.

1 W. Harrington, *A Key to the Parables* (Glen Rock N.J.: Paulist Press 1964); [*He spoke in Parables* (Dublin; Helicon 1964)] *Chapter I.*

Contents

Parables Told by Jesus

NEW INSIGHTS INTO THE PARABLES

One of the better known, though briefest, of the parables of Jesus concerns a treasure which a man found in a field and in sheer joy gave up all that he had to purchase it (Mt 13:44). Of course, the original parable equates the treasure with the Kingdom of Heaven; but we may, not unreasonably, identify this great treasure with the parables themselves. Yes, here are jewels which are so often hidden in the vaster fields of the Gospels—hidden not only because they are overshadowed by more pleasing and comforting words, perhaps, but also because their real import is often missed in that they have a way of eluding precise understanding. But we are to take heart on behalf of our treasure. One major trend in parable study has been to show how the parables, if taken just as we meet them, are more understandable, revealing more than meets the eye. Moreover, much exegesis has been done on the parables to enable us to read them with a deeper appreciation of their original life-setting (*Sitz im Leben*) and literary origin. But, outweighing this is the conclusion that they are to be read by each of us as we personally hear them. This is the way Jesus intended for the original hearers of his parables, speaking them according to each person's

3

ability to *receive* (Mk 4:33). Only when each individual receives it in his or her own personal way can the message of any parable be really communicated.

We shall point out, in a later chapter, that the stress in the parable of *the Treasure in the Field* is really threefold: it lies on the great value of the treasure, the cost of total commitment, and the joy accompanying such a rich find. We, too, shall apply this division in our survey, though in a different connection. Our aim will be to show how the parables need not be bound to their immediate context but can speak freely to us of a later age. They must speak in such a way that we strive to hear not so much the exact words in which Jesus first spoke the parables, than to hear them as his living voice today. As a preliminary step, however, it may be well to decide what we mean by a "parable."

Parables

When we hear a Gospel reading at Mass begin with the words: "... and Jesus told them this parable..." we think at once that a "story" will follow rather than either a narrative about Jesus or some other point of his teaching. And we sense that this story must have a message or a moral for us (even though sometimes we admit to ourselves that we really do not get the point). But perhaps by spending a little while in the company of parables on these pages, we can be helped to get the point more often and to accept points which we may never be able to fully understand.

"He who has ears to hear, let him hear!" (Mk 4:9).

This is what Jesus called out when he taught in parables; but we must preface the invitation even here when we merely begin to define them. He calls us to attune the ears of our heart to the singular mode of thought which the word "parable" is going to demand of us. For "parable" means more than it says. The original Greek word is *parabolē*, meaning a juxtaposition or a comparison of two realities. (The German word for parable, *Gleichnis* or "likeness," conveys something of this.) A term used in classical rhetoric, the strict parable had only one point of comparison and could be described as a prolonged simile such as those prevalent in the Homeric epics. Unlike a fable or a fairy-story, it is true-to-life. It is distinct from an allegory or a prolonged metaphor, in which every detail has meaning. However, recent studies have pointed out that there should be no hard and fast rules made in the classification of Jesus' parables, because it is not inconceivable that he intended some, at least of his parables to contain both a single point and certain allegorical details.

Now, part of this flexibility comes because we cannot really say that the New Testament usage of the word *parabolē* corresponds to its classical Greek usage. In fact, in the New Testament, *parabolē* is best understood not as a Greek word but as a translation of the Hebrew word *mashal*. Both the Septuagint (the Greek version of the Old Testament) and the New Testament itself found that *parabolē* was the best word into which to render *mashal*— but, in the process, it also took on the meaning of *mashal*. And what was this meaning? In Hebrew this word had a

5

whole range of intricate meanings far beyond a mere "comparison." It could be a representation or a type, a simile or a metaphor, a maxim or proverb or pithy saying, a symbol or a riddle. It had, too, the quality of a "dark saying," something involving mystery. Once we are aware of this Old Testament background to "parable," we cannot help realizing that it is all encompassed in the New Testament usage of the term. Then we shall approach the parables with the freedom Jesus meant us to have—the freedom of the life-giving Spirit beyond the letter.

As for the immediate background of Jesus' parables, by his day the parable proper as we know it had become a fixed form in rabbinical preaching. It drew material from daily life and gave it definite set meanings: sons or servants or children or slaves or flocks represented Israel; a king or a father meant God; a feast indicated the joys of the messianic age, and a harvest the last judgment. Thus, when Jesus chose to speak in parables, he was making use of a rabbinical form very familiar to his listeners (which is one reason we can presume they understood what he was saying). But, as might be expected of such a Spirit-anointed teacher as Jesus, he took the standard meaning and created something entirely original, unique among rabbinical parables of the era in their sheer creative brilliance and living quality. Though he gave his words an unexpected, singular twist yet, in keeping with his whole mission, Jesus sought out the very humblest of everyday things and gave them immortality—a patch on an old garment, a knock on the door at midnight, little children piping.

From all that we have seen thus far, it will not surprise us that *parabolē* is indeed used in the Gospels with a great breadth of meaning. Apart from what we usually think of as parables, it is applied to various maxims, examples and metaphors used by Jesus. This is especially important when we come to try to understand the reason why Jesus used parables. When we read, "with many such parables he spoke the word to them..." or "he did not speak to them without a parable" (Mk 4:33f), "parable" here is likely any form of figurative speech, any indirect way in which Jesus tried to convey the truth of his mission. For, "human kind cannot bear very much reality," T.S. Eliot has written. Human nature can often receive in a veiled way what it could not receive directly. That Jesus understood our human condition and so tailored and tucked his message into parables is confirmed by his words in the Johannine *Last Discourse.* There Jesus tells us that he has been "speaking in figures." But, "the hour is coming when I shall no longer speak to you in figures but tell you plainly of the Father" (Jn 16:25). The word *parabolē* does not occur here (or anywhere else in John). But the word used, *paroimia*, conveys the same meaning as the "figurative speech" implied by *parabolē* in its broadest sense. Yes, through parables, Jesus tells us what it could be too hard to hear "plainly." "I have yet many things to tell you, but you cannot bear them yet" (Jn 15:21).

PARABLES TOLD BY JESUS

The Setting of the Parables

"A sower went forth to sow his seed..." (Mk 4:3; Mt 13: 3; Lk 8:5). Jesus has not only created the parables of the New Testament, he has also "sown" them in the soil of both his earthly ministry and his continuing presence in the Church today. When we look at how these parables were first "sown" we find that there are difficulties attached to discerning their exact meaning and origin. The difficulties arose in the first place because the parables were handed down in the early Church without any indication of the time or place in which Jesus first spoke them. The evangelists had to decide for themselves about where to insert them in their Gospels. And since of course Jesus did not write them down, the parables differ according to the different understanding and traditions held by those who finally did write them.

Here are some of the "signs" indicating that the parables were indeed moulded when they were included in our Gospels:

(1) The evangelists group together parables about one topic where Jesus most likely had not. (For example Lk 15 contains three parables concerning the gain of what is "lost"; Mk 4 contains three seed parables; Lk 14 links together parables about a banquet.)

(2) Parables can have different meanings in different Gospels, according to the context. (For example in Lk 15:4-7, the Lost Sheep is told to explain Jesus'

concern for the "publicans and sinners" the outcasts of society; in Mt 18:12-14, it is addressed to the early Christian community as an exhortation for concern on behalf of erring brethren. The parables of the Lamp and the Salt of the Earth are found in different places in the Synoptics and have different meanings.)

(3) There are alterations within parables in the Synoptics. For example the Tenants in the Vineyard varies in details (Mk 12:1-11; Mt 21:33-43; Lk 20:9-18). The Pounds (Lk 19:12-27) and the Talents (Mt 25:14-30) seem to be two different versions of the same. parable; likewise with the Banquet (Lk 14:16-24) and the Wedding Feast (Mt 22:1-10).

(4) Certain parables have been given conclusions from isolated sayings of Jesus which do not apply. For example, "The last will be first and the first last" (Mt 19:30; 20:16); "Many are called but few are chosen" (Mt 22:14); the whole string of maxims (Lk 16:9-13), added on to the parable of the Unjust Steward (Lk 16:1-8).

(5) Separate parables have been fused into one. (For example the parables of the Wedding Feast, the king destroying a city, and the Wedding Garment, Mt 22. 1-14, cf Lk 14:16-24.)

(6) Some of Jesus' parables—or even his original explanations of them—were not understood by his listeners, so that the early Church has given its own "homily"

on them. (For example the interpretation of the Sower, Mk 4:13-20; Mt 13:18-23; Lk 8:11-15; and the interpretation of the Weeds, Mt 13:36-43.)

Look at the whole of Mt 13, which contains no less than seven parables of the kingdom, or Mt 24-25! Matthew, the most "architectural" of the evangelists, has clearly created two parable discourses—the first as Jesus' defense of his mission against the Jews and his encouragement for the disciples, the second as his eschatological discourse. Likewise, the bulk of Mk 4 is carefully constructed to set forth Mark's own theory of parables.

In short, scientific biblical study dealing with the parables' text, literary form and the contribution of the evangelists have made it clear that the parables have always a twofold and often a threefold, historical setting: the earthly life of Jesus, the setting in the life of the early Church, and an evangelist's editorial setting. The first setting entails what words Jesus actually used and what his original hearers understood by them. The second concerns what words the first Christians heard, and what they understood by them, when the parables had been handed down to them by oral tradition. The third setting comes into question when an evangelist deliberately fits a parable into his own editorial plan in keeping with his own theological outlook.

While it is gratifying to discern the first historical setting of a parable (in the ministry of Jesus), to press the purely academic search for the original too far is to miss the nature of the parables as an *art* form which can speak to persons of any era. Likewise, to try to confine their meanings to a single point is to impoverish them of the more general spiritual truths which Jesus surely intended them to convey. And so the *Sitz im Leben* of the early Church is equally as valid: human folk remain consistently the same! The way in which the early Christians understood a parable is a guideline for the way in which Jesus meant us too to receive his message. And the specific understanding of an evangelist reminds us that we cannot do without theology and assures us that, from the beginning, creative theologians have played a major role in the Church. Indeed, we may say that there are no limits on the meaning of a parable precisely because of its human and aesthetic elements. Jesus himself would want his parables to be set free from the confines of one *Sitz im Leben* to live each its own life amidst peoples of later ages and situations. The voice in which he first spoke them must remain abidingly alive.

The Value of the Treasure

We are now ready to return to our "parable" of the Treasure. The man who "finds" the Kingdom of heaven as if, Mt 13:44 tells us, it were a treasure hidden in a field is clearly attracted by the great value of his find. Hence, let us look first at the immense value which the parables of Jesus have for us—precisely as windows into that Kingdom. The interpretation of a goodly number of individual parables reveals different aspects of the Kingdom; we may here consider how the parables taken as a whole convey that most

11

marvelous aspect of Jesus' Good News which proclaims that this Kingdom is right here in our midst and within our hearts (Lk 17:21). For it has been pointed out, we as disciples of Jesus have already found *our* treasure because he himself has brought it to us in his person. We are to approach the parables as persons who need to stand by our treasure and guard it with steadfast conviction.

Both past and contemporary studies on the parables consistently indicate their value in making the Kingdom immediate to us through their portrayal of daily life. These stories of Jesus are unique in that they convey the vibrance of Everyday in the simplest of terms; they are filled with a clarity of vision—Jesus' own—which has cherished all ordinary things and persons in creation. This becomes especially true when we consider that many of the parables are Jesus' defense on behalf of those who are the outcasts of society—indeed, his *apologia* in face of his opponents who made *him* the chief outcast. And no formal doctrines to be derived from the parables can quite equal the lessons they teach just through their plain human appeal. Awareness of these facts has led contemporary scholars to warn against severely historical or theological interpretations of the parables which exclude or ignore the basic human needs they contain. It is the human element which constitutes the real richness of the parables (not to mention the entire incarnational import of the Man who spoke them).

Closely connected with this is another great value emerging from the parables—namely, their function of proclaiming general truths through their very human and particular details. In the past, the prolific arguments over the question of whether or not Jesus himself used allegory, tended to leave them hidebound and bereft of all meanings save a single point (tailored to fit whatever current theory or interpretation). Likewise, purely historical criticism tended to relegate them to a single context, and hence to a singular message. By contrast, recent New Testament criticism has come to the rescue of the parables and shows them just as they are through giving due weight to every aspect and detail of them. They are representational stories which *can* convey manifold truths. The parables have been freed to speak for themselves, as it were, through a more flexible approach to their interpretation. Indeed, certain hard and fast attitudes in the past have tended to deny the value of traditional meanings found in the parables in favor alone of their *original* message and setting. Now, however, the trend of study shows not only the difficulty of determining this original lifesetting of Jesus' parables, but also the fact that the traditional adaptation of each parable throughout the centuries may very likely represent its authentic message. In other words, the individual responses of the Christian heart to the parables may well be trustworthy.

Thus, though granted some of the parables which Jesus spoke *are* limited by their historical reference and some bear the didactic intention of a single lesson, for the most part they are capable of an ever-expanding meaning in terms of more general religious truths and wider applications to spiritual life. Jesus himself surely intended this—

a point *academia* cannot overlook. For, in the parables, he was not (explicitly) delivering information about his own coming, his personal life and milieu; rather he was proclaiming the vast possibility of "life more abundantly" opened out to all in the world because he *had* come (cf. Jn 10:10). Thus, there has been a recent impetus to ferret out what is abidingly relevant in the parables, the elements having a permanent significance which can be re-translated for every age and need of the Church. Like all narratives dealing with the human situation, the parables do contain what is temporary and particular. But, beyond that, they have a personal and universal relevance—that which makes them stories rather than history (or, to use Johannine terms, words of "spirit and life" rather than of "flesh"). The task of the biblical theologian and preacher is to set this relevance free for all the "little people" in the Church who need it—and who alone can really discern it!

It follows, then, that what must be discerned as normative and central in the parables, as distinct from what is passing and peripheral, enters the realm of faith. As appealing as the pictorial elements in each are, these are really in the end impossible to re-translate or adapt to modern circumstances precisely because, as we shall see, the parable is an art form. But the faith content of the parables, their revelation of what believing existence must mean, is translatable—and hence is their greatest value. A common structure of faith underlines the message of each, namely, the wider Proclamation of Jesus himself, or, indeed, the nature of God as manifested in the entire Bible. This structure of faith is comprised ultimately of the truths which form our Christian *credo.*

The parables, then, are to be seen not merely as stories which are pleasant or intriguing to read or hear, but far more as witnesses to the teaching of Jesus. For he, in the end, is the reason for our reading the parables at all! This becomes very clear in the collection known as the *Servant Parables,* because they contain a call to a special watchfulness for his coming—his coming both at the "end-time" and at any time here-and-now in all our lives. Indeed, these parables are a most valuable treasure too because the very servant metaphor in them should correct modern notions of man's autonomy before God. At the same time, according to Palestinian custom, this master-servant relationship must be seen as something as intimately personal as that between father and son.

These, then, are some of the values of our parable riches. They are truly priceless when we view the parables as a summons to decision for men in their different life-situations today as much as for their original hearers. In them each person is called to decide what he will do with his life when confronted with the Gospel and with Jesus himself. Will he choose for or against the Light?... And so, once again, we return to the parables' potential for conveying general truths. In a sense, it is like the author of Psalm 78 who begins this long historical and pictorial psalm by saying that he will "open his mouth in a parable and uttter dark sayings from old" (Ps 78:2). The point is that the following verses recount all of Yahweh's deeds of

15

love on behalf of Israel—but recount them with the explicit purpose of teaching later generations of children not to forget Yahweh as did their forefathers. The "parable" yields this deeper truth. So, too, with the parables of Jesus: born in definite historical circumstances (and at times seemingly a bit puzzling and riddlesome), yet they all somehow teach God's saving love—his love, especially, as it is manifest in Jesus.

The Cost of the Treasure

Just as in the case of *the Treasure in the Field*, the priceless treasure we find in the parables yet must be bought with a price; it carries a cost. The man who "sold all he had" to buy his treasure willingly bore the cost of total commitment or giving up all else for its sake. In our analogy of the parables as a "treasure" we can view this somewhat differently: we wish them to help us to make our commitment to Jesus more wholehearted, but there is the accompanying cost of the apparent difficulties which the parables present in regard to their understanding and interpretation. Indeed, in a sense, they are "dark sayings" or "riddles." They contain something hidden and secret which needs to be drawn out; this process, as confirmed by all studies of the parables past and present, can be demanding and costly. But we are to take heart because Jesus has given to us his disciples the special insight whereby we are able to understand them. God has disclosed his secret revelations to babes (Mt 11:25), and it concerns exactly this: that the "mystery of his Kingdom" hidden throughout the ages

16

(and throughout the parables) is made manifest in this Jesus, his Son (Col 1:26; Ep 3:8f). He, in turn, enlightens us with this insight—precisely by speaking in parables.

The nature and the cost of the treasure found in the parables is indicated in recent studies by the concern to define the role of their historical situation. Purely historical criticism of the parables strives to discern only what they conveyed to the original hearers in their concrete circumstances, as well as the reason for which Jesus first spoke each one—whether it was as encouragement for his disciples or apologetic defence before his Jewish opponents. The difficulty of discerning such an "original parable" is compounded, of course, when we accept the fact that each of the evangelists adapted the parables to his own purposes and themes (a fact underlying the science of Redaction Criticism). With the trend of recent parable studies being towards a liberation of the parables to speak for themselves, it is not surprising that scholars de-emphasize the purely historical interpretation since concentration on that alone restricts their potential freedom of application. For the same reason, a purely eschatological interpretation is unsatisfactory. Moreover, to deny the worth of the details in each parable or the possibility of allegory there is to bereave them of a richness inherent in their form. Hence, the consensus of opinion is that, while it is contained in a definite historical frame of reference, it is the *parable* which serves as interpreter of the history rather than the reverse.

In conjunction with the historical setting of the parables, much work has been done to discern their continuous "re-translation" as handed down by the Church. It is this which has shaped the parables into their present form in our Gospels, for it is the Gospels which have utilized their kerygmatic content and show how the early christian community understood them. To understand the parables through the continuous re-translation given them in their transmission down the centuries is to grasp how they continue to be Jesus' living word addressed to *every* community of *every* present moment. For, the whole force of the parables lies in their showing the listener *himself,* confronting him with his own world—indeed, even rendering that world into a "parable." The verdict of the narrator "interlocks" with that of the listener. Thus, it becomes clear that the way in which individual persons from the beginning of the Church have understood and responded to the parables does provide a valid way for discerning their authentic message. Perhaps this is because no matter how much the early kerygmatic preaching or later Christian preachers have adapted or even accommodated the parables, no one and nothing could possibly deepen their essential message. For at their heart stands Jesus himself.

It is because Jesus used his parables to meet the demands of his age that the evangelists showed through them how he continues to address living situations in later ages. Matthew 13 sets the stage for this process in a special way because its grouping of many parables shows how Jesus turns away from the Jews who had rejected him to the disciples who would receive him. This is the great "turning point" of the gospel. And so, it is up to us to approach the parables with that "pre-understanding" which is aware that here is Jesus himself, alive and speaking to us in this way by his own choice. By speaking in parables he intends to convey to us the profound reality and truth concerning the relationship between God and man as revealed in his Person. As we have tried to show, the "cost" of uncovering our hidden treasure in the parables is great because of their inherent difficulties which tend to put one off at first sight or to cloud their real import. But these difficulties, and all the complicated ins and outs of parable exegesis, would be laid to rest could we but grasp that this reality which Jesus intended to convey is not identical with the empirical, sensible world. Nor is the truth of the parables able to be tucked neatly into the envelope of theological concepts. They are a more fundamental form of expression, because they hold hands with the "little Child" who has led the whole world to redemption (Is 11:6).

The Joy in the Treasure

Having looked at the worth of our parable treasure and the costly difficulties involved in obtaining it, we turn now to that which far outweighs those difficulties and keeps us from counting the cost; the *joy* which our "find" brings to us, just as it was "in his joy" that the man of the parable sold all that he had for that field. We have mentioned that the parables are a more basic form of expression and convey a deeper truth than our usual categories allow. This follows from one special characteristic which scholars are eliciting from the parables more frequently, an aspect of them which yields their purest joy: their aesthetic appeal. For the parables *are* an art form and thus have a life of their own; and this can be their greatest advantage in the recent effort to free them to speak to people in any situation. Their sphere of reality is not identical with the empirical world because they are creations of Jesus' own vision, livened by the form and symbol his own imagination has given them.

Their characters typify all human need and experience, and this is why they speak so eloquently to us. They follow definite story-telling techniques and rules; some of them can even be called miniature plays with leading roles and changes of scenery. The parables are a more fundamental form of expression than any *concepts* in theology can convey. Born of everyday experience, yet they present a truer picture of reality than the "everyday" —that reality which can be conveyed through the medium of art. And so, it follows that just as art can speak to us only as individuals, so too the most valid interpretation of the parables can be found in our own response to them. Jesus first spoke them to persons; only each person could grasp their meanings according to the circumstances of his own life in response to Jesus. We can accept in principle that the parables are Jesus' teaching. But only in our own hearts, "hidden" as the secret of the parables, can we have "ears to hear" or "eyes to see" that there "you have seen him, and it is he who speaks to you" (Jn 9:37).

The parables, then, are an art medium; they are stories and as such open up whole pastoral realms of thought and experience for each one who reads them. This is why they are capable of an expanding meaning—and hence why confining them to any principle of interpretation, historical or otherwise, robs them of their inner richness. Here, indeed, lies the kernel of our treasure, the "pearl of great price" amidst the whole. As *art* the parables are not meant to be stagnant but reproductive; as creations, they are meant to stir the "new man" in us created by Jesus (2 Cor 5:17). An art form seeks to recapture what is abidingly relevant: this is why the characters in the parables have a universal quality and their happenings are free from time's conditioning. They are most existential and immediate because they are aesthetic; because the artistic medium on which they are based is words, a decisive event takes place through what is said.

This provides another way in which the parable is intimately bound up with the listener and with fundamental human needs. And here we find that Rudolf Bultmann's basic hermeneutical principle—that the most adequate question to be put to the Bible is what it understands human existence to be—applies particularly well to the parables. For, in his parables, Jesus was not giving information about his situation but was providing an understanding of the possibilities of existence which his situation brought. A parable dramatizes an ontological possibility (that which is possible in principle for man as man), and the two basic ontological possibilities which the parables present are the gain or loss of existence, the becoming authentic or inauthentic. At the same time, each parable depicts how existence is ontically (actually and in the concrete) gained

21

or lost as it dramatizes how the basic human possibilities or gaining or losing existence may actually occur. The aesthetic form presses the two—the ontological and the ontic—into a unity: they are integrated in one configuration of action and interpretation.

Moreover, as is evident in the parable of *the Laborers in the Vineyard,* they are also an arresting means of showing us the limitations of human existence, the imperfections in man's understanding. If the entire Bible shows the astonishing ways of God which are not those of men, if the entire Gospel is the unexpected, the parables portray this *in nuce* through their propensity for twisting situations in an intricate, unanticipated way, but a way which turns out to be the more accurate and simpler truth about the nature of the world and of man before God. Indeed, within the ordinary guise of the parables, there really is a treasure as unexpected as the one hidden in that nondescript, seemingly empty fields. The wonderful thing for us to realize is that, just as the treasure found by the man in the parable is actually the Kingdom, so too the treasures to be found in all the parables are in the service of this Kingdom. This is a clear assurance that the parables cannot have been *so* radically changed from the time Jesus first spoke them because the arrival of the Kingdom in himself was such a major part of his entire Proclamation.

Here, then, in the sheer aesthetic delight to be found in the parables as well as in the Kingdom of Jesus' message shining out from them, we find an occasion for rejoicing when we have taken the steps to procure their treasure.

Matthew concludes his 'turning point' chapter with the tiny parable of *Treasure Old and New*: every scribe trained for the Kingdom is capable of bringing both the old and the new out of his treasure—that is, he can draw upon the *whole* of God's revelation (Mt 13:52). So it is with the reader who has acquired the skill of reading Jesus' parables aright: he can perceive in their simple words, their images drawn from day-to-day life, the entire manifestation of the biblical God. But, what this Christian reader must remember is that such a skill consists in allowing the parables to speak to him personally just as he as an individual finds them. Only thus can he hear his Lord's voice in them as a *living* voice.

And Jesus does so yearn for us to hear it as such. After he has spoken many parables to the disciples and indicated to them that, as his followers, they have been given the special insight to perceive, he questions them, "Have you *understood* all this?" (Mt 13:51). The parables provide another occasion for him to express the sensitive hunger he felt throughout his life for the followers who loved him to understand and perceive who he really was. "Do you not yet perceive or understand? Are your hearts hardened? Having eyes do you not see and having ears do you not hear?..." (Mk 8:17-21). Let us try to meet his cry for understanding through harkening to all the helpful insights these recent studies on the parables have given us; they all somehow conclude that what is needful is a harkening to the parables themselves.

CHAPTER II

PARABLES IN MARK 4

1. Again he began to teach beside the sea. And a very large crowd gathered about him, so that he got into a boat and sat in it on the sea; and the whole crowd was beside the sea on the land. 2. And he taught them many things in parables, and in his teaching he said to them:

3. "Listen! A sower went out to sow. 4. And as he sowed, some seed fell along the path, and the birds came and devoured it. 5. Other seed fell on rocky ground, where it had not much soil, and immediately it sprang up, since it had no depth of soil; 6. and when the sun rose it was scorched, and since it had no root it withered away. 7. Other seed fell among thorns and the thorns grew up and choked it, and it yielded no grain. 8. And other seeds fell into good soil and brought forth grain, growing up and increasing and yielding thirtyfold and sixtyfold and a hundredfold."

9. And he said, "He who has ears to hear, let him hear."

10. And when he was alone, those who were about him with the twelve asked him concerning the parables. 11. And he said to them, "To you has been given the secret of the kingdom of God, but for those outside everything is in parables; 12. so that they may indeed see but not perceive, and may indeed hear but not understand; lest they should turn again and be forgiven."

13. And he said to them, "Do you not understand this

parable? How then will you understand all the parables?"
14. "The sower sows the word. 15. And these are the ones
along the path, where the word is sown; when they hear,
Satan immediately comes and takes away the word which
is sown in them. 16. And these in like manner are the ones
sown upon rocky ground, who, when they hear the word,
immediately receive it with joy; 17. and they have no root
in themselves, but endure for a while; then, when tribulation or persecution arises on account of the word, immediately they fall away. 18. And others are the ones sown
among thorns; they are those who hear the word, 19. but
the cares of the world, and the delight in riches, and the
desire for other things, enter in and choke the word, and it
proves unfruitful. 20. But those who were sown upon the
good soil are the ones who hear and accept it and bear fruit,
thirtyfold and sixtyfold and a hundredfold."

21. And he said to them, "Is a lamp brought in to be
put under a bushel, or under a bed, and not on a stand? 22.
For there is nothing hid, except to be made manifest; nor is
anything secret, except to come to light. 23. If any man
has ears to hear, let him hear."

24. And he said to them, "Take heed what you hear;
the measure you give will be the measure you get, and still
more will be given you. 25. For to him who has will more
be given; and from him who has not, even what he has
will be taken away."

26. And he said, "The kingdom of God is as if a man
should scatter seed upon the ground, 27. and should sleep
and rise night and day, and the seed should sprout and
grow, he knows not how. 28. The earth produces of itself,
first the blade, then the ear, then the full grain in the ear.
29. But when the grain is ripe, at once he puts in the sickle,
because the harvest has come."

30. And he said, "With what can we compare the

kingdom of God, or what parable shall we use for it? 31. It is like a grain of mustard seed, which, when sown upon the ground, is the smallest of all the seeds on earth; 32. yet when it is sown it grows up and becomes the greatest of all shrubs, and puts forth large branches, so that the birds of the air can make nests in its shade."

33. With many such parables he spoke the word to them, as they were able to hear it; 34. he did not speak to them without a parable, but privately to his own disciples he explained everything.

Teaching in Parables

The passage on parables (Mk 4:1-34) is complex and is composed of a number of clearly-defined sections: an introduction (1f), the parable of the Sower (3-9), and explanation of the Sower, introduced by a question (10, 13-20), a saying on the purpose of parables (11f), two parabolic sayings (21-25), the parable of the Seed Growing to Harvest (26-29), the parable of the Mustard Seed (30-32), and a concluding statement on the use of parables (33f). Its composite character emerges unmistakably: i) From a comparison of vv. 1 and 35 it would seem that Jesus had remained in the boat, teaching the crowd, and then crossed the lake in the evening; but in v. 10 he is alone with the twelve. From v. 26 on, the parables are once again addressed to the crowd. ii) The saying of vv. 11f separates the parable of the Sower (3-9) from its explanation (13-20). iii) The interpretation of the Sower (13-20) and the parabolic sayings (21-25) are each introduced by the typical Marcan link-formula, "and he said to them" (vv. 13, 21,

24). iv) The question of v. 10 receives two answers, each introduced by the introductory formula (vv. 11f, 13-20).

We may, with some confidence, form a general picture of how 4:1-34 was built up. The primitive tradition combined the three parables (3-9, 26-29, 30-32); at an early stage the explanation of the Sower (13-20), introduced by the question (v. 10), was supplied. Vv. 33a, 34a ("With many such parables he spoke the word to them; he did not speak to them without a parable") could well have been the conclusion of this complex; vv. 33b, 34b ("as they were able to hear it"; "but privately to his own disciples he explained everything") is Mark's modification of the conclusion to bring it into line with his theory of the purpose of parables. The evangelist himself added the other answer (11f) to the question of v. 10, and the parabolic sayings (21-23, 24f)—the introductory formula clearly indicates his hand. These passages (11f, 21-23, 24f) are, all three of them, reflections on the teaching in parables as such; they are editorial additions. They explain, from Mark's point of view, why Jesus spoke in parables. Finally, his introduction (vv. 1f) provides a setting for the teaching in parables. Besides all this he has retouched, or more truly, composed, vv. 10 and 13. Whatever the accuracy in detail of this reconstruction, it is undoubtedly true that the material in the section is varied. This is an important factor in our study of it.

We may ask why the evangelist assembled the material and edited the passage for insertion in his Gospel just at this point. It would seem that the parables are meant to give

28

an assurance of the triumph of the Kingdom of God despite the gathering storm of hostility. In 2:1-3:6 Mark had given examples of the hostility offered to Jesus, hostility which ended in the cross. But since it is God's Messiah who is thus opposed and rejected, then this opposition and rejection are not final. The purpose of God can be discerned in them and the last word must be victory, not defeat. Thus the parables, and the sayings which accompany them, are not narrated at this point in order to give typical examples of Jesus' teaching but serve a particular purpose: they are intended to give his own explanation of the meaning of his ministry. These varied parables and sayings strike one note: ultimate success in spite of manifold hindrance.[1]

This verdict does indeed cover the parables and the parabolic sayings, and it brings out the ultimate ineffectiveness of the opposition to Jesus. The rest of the material (vv. 10-20, 33f) offers a theological analysis of that opposition. Already in the parables, the importance of "hearing" is stressed (vv. 3, 9, 23f); now it is seen that this "hearing" stands in contrast to a "hearing but not understanding" (v. 12). Consequently, there is a withdrawing from "those outside" (v. 11), who do not understand, and a turning to those who will receive the "secret of the kingdom" (vv. 11, 34). In the explanation of the Sower the two levels of understanding are illustrated: the superficial level, of "seeing" and "hearing" (v. 12) is exemplified by those who "hear" the word but then fall away (vv. 15, 16, 18). The deeper level, called "perceiving" and "understanding" (v. 12)—and explanation aimed at bringing these about (v.

29

PARABLES TOLD BY JESUS

20). It is significant that none other than Satan (v. 15) blocks the transition from the first level of understanding to the second; he achieves his purpose through tribulation and persecution (v. 17) and the cares and lures of the world (v. 19). Those who attain the second level of understanding receive it as a gift from God (v. 11)—the passive form "has been given" implies God as the agent. Once again, we see Satan and the Spirit-filled Messiah locked in struggle (cf. 1:12f); the words of Jesus, too, are weapons in his warfare on God's behalf.[2]

The Purpose of Parables

10. And when he was alone, those who were about him with the twelve asked him concerning the parables. 11. And he said to them, "To you has been given the secret of the kingdom of God, but for those outside everything is in parables; 12. so that they may indeed see but not perceive, and may indeed hear but not understand; lest they should turn again, and be forgiven" (4:10-12).

The brief passage 4:10f is of great importance. It is a key text for Mark's doctrine of the Messianic Secret (the truth that the Messiah can be known for who he truly is only on the other side of death and resurrection) and, in the light of this doctrine, it reveals his special theory on the use of parables. Signs of compilation are not wanting. The saying of vv. 11f is introduced by the Marcan link-formula, "And he said to them"; and, in v. 10, the phrase, "those who were about him with the twelve" is certainly awkward. It is clear, in fact, that v. 10 was originally a

30

question leading naturally and immediately to the explanation of the parable (13-20). It seems probable that the saying referred to the teaching of Jesus in general and was inserted here by Mark—in view of the word "parables," yes, but mainly because of his own theology. The evangelist is preoccupied with the problem of the Jewish hostility to and rejection of Jesus; he sees it as, in some fashion, falling under the deliberate decree of God. And so, in his eyes, teaching in parables, being enigmatic, veils the truth from those who are not meant to have it. But Jesus will instruct in the full meaning of the parables those who are meant to receive the divine gift of the truth.

The phrase, "And when he was alone" (4:10), which does not agree with vv. 1f, prepares the setting for vv. 11f. "Alone" (*kata monas*) is a synonym of the characteristic Marcan phrase *kat' idian*, "privately," "by themselves" (cf. 4:34; 6:31f; 7:33; 9:2,28; 13:3). Each time the expression is used in connection with a revelation or a private teaching reserved for the disciples. "Those who were about him with the twelve"—in the immediate context this group corresponds to the "you" and stands in contrast to the "those outside" of v. 11. Mark is, in reality, reflecting the life and experience of his Christian community; Christians are those who understand, they are not "those outside." Furthermore, the readers of this gospel are in some manner present among the hearers of Jesus—they are represented by "those about him." It is generally agreed that the original text would have referred to the parable of the Sower; by using the plural ("the parables") Mark adapts it to introduce his own parable theory. Thus it emerges that an un-explained parable is as much an enigma to the disciples as to the crowds. It is evident that editorial work in v. 10 has been extensive. We can take it that in the evangelist's source it would have been a simple introduction to the explanation of the Sower (14-20): the twelve asked him concerning the parable. Mark has completely rewritten the verse.

It will be necessary to take vv. 11f singly, but first it is helpful to consider them together and see what Joachim Jeremias has made of them.[3] We need to recall the wide range of the Hebrew word *mashal* which stands behind "parable" in the gospels. Then we find in v. 11 a contrast between the disciples ("to you") and the others ("those outside"), and according to the rules of parallelism—which apply in this case—the same contrast should exist between "secret" (literally, "mystery") and "parable"; this parallel does exist when *parabolē* is given the quite regular meaning of its Hebrew equivalent: "riddle," "a dark saying." We now have the required antithesis: to you the secret is revealed—those outside are confronted by riddles; and we may render the second half of v. 11: "But for those outside all things are obscure."

V. 12 is a free quotation of Is 6:9f. This grim declaration must be understood in its Hebrew idiom. It is not God who blinds men to the truth; that blindness is their own fault. What the text really says is that God clearly foresees that the people will not listen to his prophet—a study of the Gospels can surely convince us that the passage can be fittingly applied to Jesus and his teaching. The phrase "in order that" which introduces the quotation is a conventional abbreviation, and the full introductory formula would read: "In order that the Scripture might be fulfilled, which says. . . ." The passive "has been given" (cf. also v. 12, "be forgiven") is a circumlocution for "God"— the Jews of the time sought to avoid mention of the name of God whenever possible; Jesus seems to have commonly followed the convention. We may render the passage as follows:

To you has God given the secret of the kingdom of God, but for those outside everything is obscure; in order that (as it is written) "they may indeed see but not perceive, and may indeed hear and yet not understand, unless they turn and God will forgive them."

The saying deals not with parables but with the Lord's teaching in general. It concerns the "secret of the kingdom" which is revealed to the disciples and not to all. What is this secret? It is in fact that the kingdom is already present in the person of Jesus and in his works. By dint of patient teaching the disciples had arrived at a realization of this truth (a realization that was very imperfect until the great light of the resurrection had shone upon it), but the people had quite failed to recognize the signs of the times (Lk 12:54-59). It is, no doubt, in view of the Jewish rejection of Jesus—the terrible blindness of Israel of which Paul speaks—that the saying was remembered in the early Church. Mark is here reflecting that not even the parables had won over the hearers to faith. But a main point is the

33

special formation which the disciples, and they alone, had received.

This explanation of the verses is instructive and affords a number of valuable insights. However, it fails to take cognizance of the theological contribution of Mark—here, and throughout the whole passage. The saying of 11f, introduced by the Marcan link-formula, is an editorial insertion between the (original) question about the meaning of the Sower and its interpretation in 14-20. It is concerned with the purpose of the parabolic form as such.[4] "To you" —that is "those who were about him with the twelve" (v. 10): the disciples, and by extension, the Christian readers of the gospel. In the gospel of Mark the messianic secret is a literary procedure designed to propound a special theological viewpoint; his readers thus take their place among the immediate disciples of Jesus and share a revelation in which "those outside" have no part. "The secret of the kingdom of God"—literally, "the mystery (*mystērion*) of the kingdom of God." Here Mark gives a descriptive title to his messianic secret: it is a "mystery." The word *raz*, "mystery," is found in the late Old Testament writings. In Daniel (2:19, 28-30) it designates the eschatological plan of God, in particular the coming of the eternal Kingdom which will bring to an end all the ephemeral empires of men. Yet, Mark has specified that it is *the* secret (mystery) itself which is given to the disciples, and that "everything happens in parables" (cf Mt/Lk). Thus, for him, the events themselves are "parables"; that is, they are signs and figures of eschatological realities. The eschatolo-

34

gical reality itself is given to the disciples; they already participate in its mysterious realization.

However, the Pauline use of "mystery" is of particular relevance. We find that for Paul the "mystery"—long kept secret by God but now "made manifest to his saints" (Col 1:26)—is identified with the person of Jesus Christ (Ep 3:4; Col 4:3; 1 Tm 3:16) and, at the same time, is identical with the Gospel: the proclamation of the Gospel *is* the mystery which was kept secret for long ages (Rm 16:25; cf Ep 3:1-9; 6:19). We find that for Mark, too, while the content of the mystery is the kingdom of God (1:14f; 4:11), the presence of the kingdom in the person of Jesus, the "mystery" which he proclaims, is "the word" (4:33; cf 2:2), that is, the Gospel; Mark can identify Jesus with the Gospel at 8:35 and 10:29. Thus, the mystery which has been given to the disciples involves above all an understanding of the person of Jesus. "Everything is in parables" —literally, "everything happens in parables" "everything" is the content of the "mystery." The privileged disciples (and the readers) know the secret of the kingdom, but the others perceive nothing; the whole economy of the kingdom remains incomprehensible to "those outside." "Everything happens in parables" explains to the disciples—and the readers—why Jesus speaks of himself and of the kingdom in parables, and only in parables (v. 34). Clearly, for Mark, *parabolē* has a meaning close to "riddle."

The citation, in v. 12, of Is 6:9f follows the *Targum*, the Aramaic paraphrastic version. In its Isaiah setting the saying is a forceful and paradoxical way of proclaiming

35

what is inevitably going to happen: the prophet's preaching will not be heeded. This text was applied by the early Christians in a sense very close to its original significance (see the parallel passages Mt 13:14f; Lk 8:10). In Jn 12:40 it describes Jewish blindness to the "signs" of Jesus; and in Ac 28:25-27, Paul applies it to the Jewish reaction to his preaching. It is evident that the Marcan logion originally had a wider scope and must have referred to the whole ministry (certainly the whole preaching) of Jesus. Jesus himself (or the primitive tradition) had noted that the proclamation of the Good News had gone unheeded (cf. Lk 19:42); the people were blind to the Gospel and had not heeded the invitation of their God. But Mark has applied this general logion to the particular case of the parables and so has given it a new meaning, in accordance with his parable theory. This theory he has expressed in vv. 11 and 33b, 34b: Jesus speaks clearly only to his immediate disciples; to those outside he speaks only in parables so that they will not understand. V. 12 is a Scripture quotation which illustrates this theory.

We are at the heart of the messianic secret: it is precisely a question of the link which exists between the present activity of Jesus and the establishment of the kingdom of God.[5] The truth is that the kingdom is already present, present in him, in his works and words. But, for the moment (cf. vv. 21f) only the disciples of Jesus can understand—and even they need to be taught (v. 34). For the others, those outside, "everything happens in parables";

without God's gift of revelation (v. 11) all remains incomprehensible. And this state of affairs has been willed by God (v. 12), but provisionally (vv. 21f) and for a special reason which is not yet disclosed.

It is, obviously, a matter of importance to understand what Mark means by "parable." His association of "mystery" and "parable" in v. 11 suggests the apocalyptic tradition; it does seem that the *Book of Enoch* (Jewish composite writing of roughly between 170 and 60 B.C.) is instructive. In the parable section of this work (chs. 37-71), the visions concerning the heavenly "mysteries" are revealed to Enoch in three great parables; the word "parable" appears at the head of each of the three sections of this part of the book (38:1; 45:1; 58:1). An editorial note in 68:1 closely associates "mysteries" and "parables": "And after that my grandfather Enoch gave me the teaching of all the secrets [mysteries] in the book in the parables which had been given to him"—the "parables" are the vehicles of the "mysteries." In Enoch, it is important to note, the parables concern the heavenly realities which it is not given to man to perceive, without a special revelation; the seer himself has to have his vision explained to him (46:2). It would appear that Mark, in view of his parable theory, chose to regard the parables of Jesus in a similar light. Certainly, this is what emerges from Mk 4: 11. The parables of Jesus reveal, to the privileged few, the mystery of the kingdom of God, a mystery hidden from all up to the present, and now revealed by God to those whom

37

he has chosen. And indeed, with regard to content, the parables of Jesus are not unlike the apocalyptic parables. In them, too, the events of the Judgment are revealed, and the establishment of the kingdom of God. They are the revelation of heavenly realities, realities which no one can understand without a spontaneous and gratuitous revelation of God.

It seems clear that Mark made use of a little collection of parables he had to hand in order to present and illustrate his own theory of the messianic secret. He sees the parables of Jesus as, in some fashion, similar to the apocalyptic parables and, by the same token, associated with the apocalyptic "mystery." Jesus' parables contain the secret of the divine revelation, a mystery whose meaning awaits a full definite manifestation. We should, however, take care to observe that if Mark affirms that Jesus speaks in parables "so that they may not understand," he also explains that this state of affairs is only for a short while (4:21f); in a word, 4:11f and 4:21f are complementary. If we take together the editorial additions of Mark in this chapter we discern his particular viewpoint: Jesus speaks to the crowds in "parables," to veil from them the mystery of the Kingdom—it is a way of indicating that the strange obduracy of Israel is still somehow part of God's design. It is a thoroughly "biblical" way of dealing with such a problem. But, as in his presentation, the disciples, too, fail to understand, he points out that this situation is provisional; in a little while the mystery will be proclaimed everywhere

(4:21f). In the meantime, Jesus is content to explain the meaning of his words to his intimate disciples alone.

Parabolic Sayings 4:21-25

21. And he said to them, "Is a lamp brought in to be put under a bushel, or under a bed, and not on a stand? 22. For there is nothing hid, except to be made manifest; nor is anything secret, except to come to light."
23. "If any man has ears to hear, let him hear."
24. And he said to them, "Take heed what you hear; the measure you give will be the measure you get, and still more will be given you. 25. For to him who has will more be given; and from him who has not, even what he has will be taken away."

The parable of the Sower and its Explanation will be studied in a later chapter. We turn now to 4:21-25, a passage built up of five separate logia arranged in the pairs 21f and 24f, with v. 23 as a connecting link relating them to the Sower (cf. 4:9). The formula, "And he said to them" (vv. 21, 24), indicates that they are Marcan insertions; this formula also suggests that the sayings already stood in pairs.

Similarity of subject matter links the sayings of vv. 21f. For Mark, the resultant "parable" clarifies his viewpoint expressed in 4:11f. Just as it is the true function of a lamp to give light, so the parables of Jesus are meant to enlighten; this is their ultimate purpose. The "hid" and "secret" of v. 22 recall the "mystery" of v. 11; it is conceded that the mystery of the kingdom is hidden for a time—but only for a time. What is now hidden will eventually be revealed to all. The evangelist's meaning probably is that though the mystery of the kingdom was hidden during the ministry of Jesus, it was destined to be proclaimed abroad after the resurrection (cf. 9:9). The mystery has been hidden with the disciples in order that they may make it known. Of course, this meaning is rather forced and artificial because these sayings are really isolated logia and their present context is certainly not original (cf., for v. 21, Lk 11:33; Mt 5:15, and for v. 22, Lk 12:1; Mt 10:26). The solemn warning of 4:23 echoes 4:9; here it is meant to emphasize the responsibility of disciples. It underlines the message of vv. 21f and suggests "that it contains an important truth, needful for the times in which Mark is writing: the time has now come to abandon the policy of reserve, and to proclaim the Gospel plainly before men!"[6]

The second pair of sayings (vv 24f) is far more obscure and difficult. "Take heed what you hear" means, carefully consider what you hear; weigh its meaning. It is necessary to give all one's attention to Jesus' parables, in order the better to understand their meaning. The proverbial saying (v. 24b) gives the reason for heeding. This saying occurs in Mt 7:2, and Lk 6:38 in a context of judgment: you will be judged in the measure you judge others, and it is obviously at home in that context. But Mark sets it in relation to the parables and its sense, for him, seems to be: your attention to the teaching will be the measure of the profit you will receive from it. The second saying (v. 25) may have been a popular proverb. The other synoptists have the saying again after the *parable of the Talents/Pounds* (Mt 25:29; Lk 19:26): Jesus would have applied the proverb to spiritual things. Here Mark seemingly takes it to mean that the spiritual insight which denotes openness to the teaching of Jesus (v. 24) will be deepened by God (the passive, "will be given," implies God as the agent); and, conversely, indifference to the message of the parable will lead to a loss of whatever insight one may have had.

It is obvious that none of these sayings originally referred to the parabolic teaching of Jesus. Mark has chosen to connect them with his own parable theory. His insertion of them here makes that much clear at least; for the rest, we cannot be sure of the *precise* meaning they had for him.

The Seed Growing to Harvest 4:26-29

26. And he said, "The kingdom of God is as if a man should scatter seed upon the ground, 27. and should sleep and rise night and day, and the seed should sprout and grow, he knows not how. 28. The earth produces of itself, first the blade, then the ear, then the full grain in the ear. 29. But when the grain is ripe, at once he puts in the sickle, because the harvest has come."

This parable is peculiar to Mark. We do not know the original context of it and so there must be some doubt as to its interpretation. It seems best to take it as a parable of contrast—a contrast between the inactivity of the sower and the certainty of the harvest.

"And he said" (v. 26)—this short, indeterminate

phrase (not "and he said *to them*") occurs in 4:9, 26, 30 and nowhere else in Mark. Furthermore, it is found only within the heart of the parable passage, the little collection of three parables: it links the saying of v. 9 to the Sower (3-8) and then joins on the other parables, the Seed Growing to Harvest (26-29) and the Mustard Seed (30-32). It is not, then, editorial, but is part of the traditional nucleus taken over by the evangelist. The kingdom of God is not compared ultimately to the seed but to the harvest. And just as in 4:3, the sower initiates a process; his subsequent inactivity is a main point of the parable.

The sower goes his way; his life follows its normal ordered round (v. 27). All the while the seed sprouts and grows without his taking anxious thought. In fact, there is nothing the sower can do because "the earth produces of itself"—this is very emphatically stated (v. 28). The seed grows from blade, to ear, to full corn: its growth is irresistible. Then, one day, the time again comes for the intervention of the farmer (v. 29). The grain is ripe and "at once" he proceeds to harvest it. The citation of Joel 3:13 ("Put in the sickle, for the harvest is ripe") is unexpected and, indeed, awkward. It refers to the eschatological judgment (cf. Rv 14:14-20), whereas our text has in view the full harvest of the Kingdom. Besides it would suggest that he who reaps is God; in the parable the sower (who does not know how the seed grows—thus not God) and the reaper, are one and the same. The citation must be a later addition. God is the one who brings about the growth, and St Paul had learned the lesson of the parable: "I planted,

Apollos watered, but God gave the growth. So neither he who plants nor he who waters is anything, but only God who gives the growth" (1 Cor 3:6).

It may be that, originally, the parable was Jesus' reply to those who looked, impatiently, for a forceful intervention of God or of his Kingdom; or it may have been meant to give assurance to those of the disciples who were discouraged because nothing seemed to be happening. Mark, at least, takes it in the latter sense. Jesus encourages his disciples: in spite of hindrance and apathy the seed was being sown; its growth is the work of God who will bring it to harvest.

The Parable of the Mustard Seed 4:30-32

30. And he said, "With what can we compare the kingdom of God, or what parable shall we use for it? 31. It is like a grain of mustard seed, which, when sown upon the ground, is the smallest of all the seeds on earth; 32. yet when it is sown it grows up and becomes the greatest of all shrubs, and puts forth large branches, so that the birds of the air can make nests in its shade."

This is another parable of contrast; but again the idea of growth must be given due weight. The contrast between insignificant beginning and mighty achievement is primary—but the seed does *grow* into a plant.

The rabbis usually began their parables with the words: "A parable: it is like...," which was a conventional abbreviation of: "I will tell you a parable. With what may the matter be compared? It is the case with it as with...." Our text (v. 30) is quite like the rabbinical formula. Cf. Lk 13:20f. "It is the case with it (the kingdom) as with a grain of mustard seed." It follows that it is not the seed itself but what happens to the seed that is significant, and the kingdom is like the great shrub that grows out of the seed. In the Greek v. 31 is very awkward; its roughness is due, in large measure, to the explanatory parenthesis: "being, as it is, smaller than all seeds on the ground." The smallness of the mustard seed was proverbial (cf. Mt 17:20; Lk 17:6) and there would have been no need of such a parenthesis in the original Galilean setting. The note may have been added by Mark; but, more likely, it was already in his version of the parable. At any rate it is meant for non-Palestinian hearers of the parable. As the Marcan text stands, the small beginnings of the kingdom are carefully emphasized: every word depicts its smallness.

By contrast, in v. 32, every word now paints the greatness of the shrub. In favorable conditions the tiny mustard seed could grow into a shrub some eight or ten feet high. Again, v. 32a is probably explanatory, like the parenthesis of v. 31. The most primitive form of the parable is that of Q (Mt/Lk): "It is like a grain of mustard seed which a man took and sowed in his garden, and it grew and became a tree." In Mt 13:32 and Lk 13:19, the birds nest in the branches of the tree; here they roost under its shade. In Dn 4:12; Ezk 17:23; 31:6 a tree sheltering the birds is a symbol of a great empire offering protection to its subject peoples. It may be that Mark has the Gentiles in mind; the expression of the Gospel will bring all nations within the scope of the Kingdom.

The *parable of the Mustard Seed* would have been the answer of Jesus to an objection, latent or expressed: could the kingdom really come from such inauspicious beginnings? His reply is that the little cell of disciples will indeed become a kingdom. And, in the last analysis, if the kingdom does reach its full dimensions, it is not due to anything in the men who are the seed of the kingdom; the growth is due solely to the power of God (cf. 1 Cor 3:6f). That is why Jesus can speak with utter confidence of the final stage of the kingdom; and that is why the parable is a call to patience.

We find—at least this is so if we follow one interpretation of the Sower—that the three Marcan parables (3-9, 26-29, 30-32) are all parables of contrast: Jesus contrasts insignificant beginnings with the full flowering of the kingdom of God. In the Sower we are shown the harvest of the kingdom, a harvest abundant beyond expectation; the seed has grown despite weeds and birds and inhospitable soil. Jesus encourages his disciples, telling them that in spite of every failure and every hindrance, the kingdom of God grows and develops. The marvelous growth of the kingdom is the work of God; this is the message of the Seed Growing to Harvest. Just as surely as, for the farmer, after long waiting, the harvest does come, so as certainly God, when his hour has come, when the eschatological measure is full, will bring in his kingdom. In the Mustard Seed

PARABLES TOLD BY JESUS

Jesus admits that the kingdom, in its beginnings, gives no obvious promise of its range, no more than a tiny seed seems capable of growing into a tall shrub. But from that seed a tree does spring, offering its branches as shelter to the birds; and from the little band of Jesus' disciples a kingdom will grow, spreading wide and embracing all men. In this sustained contrast, Mark will have found support for his messianic secret. For the present, during the ministry of Jesus, the kingdom of God remains hidden, unknown, apparently fruitless; but, in a little while, it will be manifest in a striking fashion and all the world will see it.

The Use of Parables 4:33-34

33. With many such parables he spoke the word to them, as they were able to hear it; 34. he did not speak to them without a parable, but privately to his own disciples he explained everything.

These verses round of the section 4:1-34. There is some inconsistency between them. It seems reasonable to regard 33a and 34a as the conclusion of the primitive collection of parables, while 33b and 34b reflect Mark's parable theory.

"With many such parables" (v. 33)—the parables just given are only a selection, a few out of many. "The word" is the good news of the kingdom, as in 2:2. "As they were able to hear"—adapted to the capacity of the hearers. The whole verse might be taken as putting neatly both the fact of Jesus' use of parables and the purpose of his preaching in parables. Yet, the final phrase seems to be Mark's way of suggesting that the hearers could understand only a part of the teaching in parables.

The first part of v. 34 does more than repeat in negative form the positive statement in v. 33; it affirms that Jesus spoke *only* in parables to the crowds. Indeed, from the whole verse it emerges that he refused to address the crowd in any other way and reserved explicit teaching for his disciples alone. While it must be admitted that Mt 13:34 has the same idea, yet, in the light of Mk 4:11f one cannot fail to discern Mark's special position according to which the "parable" is a deliberately obscure literary form whose meaning must be specially revealed. This becomes explicit in v. 34b; the phrase *kat' idian,* "privately," we have seen, always, in Mark, indicates a revelation or a private teaching reserved for the disciples (cf. 4:10). In view of these factors, and taking account of Mark's extensive editorial contribution throughout this section, we should regard v. 34b as his own composition. Together with v. 33b it clearly reflects his theological outlook and concludes what he has to say about the use of parables by Jesus.

(1) R.H. Lightfoot, *The Gospel Message of St. Mark* (O.U.P. 1950), 39f.
(2) J. M. Robinson, *The Problem of History in Mark* (London: SCM 1957), 77.
(3) J. Jeremias, *The Parables of Jesus* (London: SCM 1963²), 15-18.
(4) G. Minette de Tillesse, *Le Secret Messianique dans l'Evangile de Marc* (Paris: Cerf 1968), 165-221.
(5) The Gospel of Mark is built up of two complementary parts. The first (1:14-8:30) is concerned with the mystery of Jesus' identity; it is dominated by the question, "Who is Jesus?" The second part (8:31-16:8) is concerned with the mysterious messianic destiny of

PARABLES TOLD BY JESUS

Jesus. The *secrecy* motif, at least in the direct form of the imposition of silence, is found only in the first part of the gospel. The motif of the *incomprehension* of the disciples, on the other hand, spans both parts of the gospel and is integral to both actions. Thus the motifs, though related, are distinct. The disciples' lack of understanding prevails to the end and is even more prominent in the second part than in the first. The insistence on secrecy can lessen and disappear in the second part as it becomes clearer and clearer that the path of Jesus lies in one direction.

The *identity* of Jesus and the *nature* of his messiahship—these are the themes of the first and the second parts of the Gospel respectively, and they are the stuff of the messianic secret. "Those outside" (4:11), "they" (4:33f), "men" (8:27) are those who are hardhearted and who will not understand or accept the person of Jesus, his messiahship: they represent Israel who rejected his message and himself. They do not grasp the inner meaning of his parables—God has not revealed it to them because they are not receptive. In regard to his miracles they did not "see signs" (cf Jn 6:26): they did not perceive the true significance of his works. The imposition of silence after the miracles makes that point: the bystanders have not understood, therefore they are to keep silent (cf Mk 1:44; 5:43; 7:36; 8:26). That the demons are forbidden to divulge his identity (1:34; 3:12), is perhaps meant to underline the fact that his exorcisms were a manifestation of his messiahship even though the demons alone were able to recognize this.

Twice (8:30 and 9:9) silence is enjoined on the disciples, but each time the situation is different. In the first case (8:30) they have perceived and acknowledged his messiahship. In the other case (9:9) they are given the limit of that silence: "Until the Son of man should have risen from the dead." However, the resurrection marks not only the limit of the secret: it lies at the center of their failure to understand (9:10). Until they had recognized Jesus as Messiah they had nothing to reveal. But they are not yet ready to preach him: they must learn what his suffering, death and resurrection mean before they can give a true picture of him. The imposition of secrecy on the disciples is not permanent. Indeed, it will be their duty to proclaim not only the messianic identity of Jesus but also the nature of his messiahship—but will be beyond the Cross and the Resurrection. Half-way through the gospel they discover the answer to the question, "Who is Jesus?" (8:29). And the gospel closes with the message (16:7) that will open their eyes to the full reality of his person.

(6) A.E.J. Rawlinson, *The Gospel According to St Mark* (London: Methuen 1925).

CHAPTER III

PARABLES IN MATTHEW 13

The pivotal position of chapter 13 in Matthew's gospel, and its emphasis on parables and their interpretation, make the chapter a crucial test of the redaction-critical method of gospel study—the analysis of an evangelist's specific contribution. We shall study the chapter and its over-all significance; at the end we shall assume that, in broad lines at least, Matthew's aims and interests have been accurately discerned.[1] And what we do find is that just as Jesus used parables to meet the demands of his own situation, so does Matthew use them to meet the needs of the community, the church, to which he belonged. He has put the parables of ch. 13 in the service of his own age and of his own theology.

We need to glance at the context of Mt 13. It turns out that the parable section forms the second part of the coherent whole 11:2-13:53. Part one (chs. 11-21) records the mounting opposition to Jesus and the rejection of him by the leaders of the people. This is underlined by the words of thanksgiving for the revelation to "babes" of what remains hidden to the "wise and understanding" (11: 23f), and culminates in the passage about the "true relatives" of Jesus, those who do the will of the Father (12:46-

50). Then, in 13:1-35, Jesus addresses "the crowds" as representing the whole of unbelieving Judaism (cf. chs. 11-12); those who are blind, deaf, lacking understanding (13:10-13). Thus, Matthew is saying that the first half of Jesus' parable discourse is an apologia; it is his reaction to his having been rejected by the Jews. But the second half of the discourse (13:36-52) marks a sudden shift to the *disciples* (13:36). They are such as do God's will (13:49-50). Jesus instructs them as to what doing God's will really means.

Parables

At least in his chapter 13, Matthew's use of *parable* seems to conform to that of Mark in two aspects. Matthew regards the parable as an enigmatic form of speech directed primarily at outsiders. He distinguishes between a time when Jesus addressed the Jews openly and a time when he begins to address them in parables. In particular, he suggests that Jesus' reply to his rejection by the Jews was distinctively parabolic in form. Jesus had come to the Jews, preaching and teaching, but was rejected by them. He reacted by addressing his apologia to them—but in parables, that is, in riddle, in speech for outsiders. By this fact he proclaims that the Jews are no longer the privileged people of God but, rather, stand under judgment for having spurned their Messiah. This factor (Jesus' turning from the Jews and towards his disciples) is the great turning-point of the Gospel; Matthew uses his parable chapter to mark the turning-point. But, for him, this is not a matter of past history: it has immediate relevance for the church to which he belongs. It reflects the relationship, one of virulent animosity, between the Church and contemporary Pharisaic Judaism. However, it is important to realize that Matthew's own community incorporated both Jews and Gentiles. For, while the evangelist does consider the leaders of Pharisaic Judaism to be incorrigible, radically closed to the saving message of Jesus, the same does not hold true for the Jewish people as such. The people of the Jews may still be evangelized and the Gospel is addressed to them.

In chapter 13, Matthew called attention to the great turning-point in several ways. Thus, he studiously avoids designating Jesus' speech in parables to the Jews as teaching (*didaskein*) or preaching (*keryssein*); instead he describes it as *lalein*, that is, a "speaking." Furthermore, Matthew consistently refers to the Jewish crowds in 13:1-35 as "them" (*autois*); he thereby depicts the (unbelieving) Jews as a people that stands outside the circle of those to whom God imparts his revelation and promises his end-time Kingdom. He introduced the term *parabolē* for the first time in chapter 13 and then distinguishes between a time when Jesus spoke openly to the Jews and a time when he spoke to them enigmatically. Finally, he gathered eight parabolic units (and two explanations), provided a framework for them, and so drifted a parable speech in two parts.

The guiding factor in Matthew's use of parabolic speech is the immediate objective he desires any given parable or series of parables to serve. All the parables of ch.

51

PARABLES TOLD BY JESUS

13 are explicitly designated as parables about the Kingdom of heaven. The closing periscope of the parable chapter tells us that, through Jesus' speech in parables, the disciples have been instructed about the Kingdom; that the instruction has met with understanding on the part of the disciples; that such understanding has for its object the doing of God's will. Indeed, it emerges that the knowing and doing of God's will is the unifying thought behind Mt 13. Matthew develops this thought negatively by depicting the Jews as those who neither know nor do God's will. Positively, he depicts the disciples (representing the Church of his day) as those who do know and do the will of God. In short, "Matthew employs parables of Jesus in order that Jesus Kyrios, who lives in the midst of his Church, can address himself to the situation of the Church's own day. This reveals that Matthew conceives Jesus' parabolic tradition as a living tradition, for through it Jesus directs, teaches, and exhorts Christians of a later age."[2]

Part I. 13:1-35

1. That same day Jesus went out of the house and sat beside the sea. 2. And great crowds gathered about him, so that he got into a boat and sat there; and the whole crowd stood on the beach. 3. And he told them many things in parables, saying:
"A sower went out to sow. 4. And as he sowed, some seed fell along the path, and the birds came and devoured them. 5. Other seeds fell on rocky ground, where they had not much soil, and immediately they sprang up, since they had no depth of soil, 6. but when the sun rose they were

scorched; and since they had no root they withered away. 7. Other seeds fell upon thorns, and the thorns grew up and choked them. 8. Other seeds fell on good soil and brought forth grain, some a hundredfold, some sixty, some thirty. 9. He who has ears, let him hear."

10. Then the disciples came and said to him, "Why do you speak to them in parables?" 11. And he answered them, "To you it has been given to know the secrets of the kingdom of heaven, but to them it has not been given. 12. For to him who has will more be given, and he will have abundance; but from him who has not, even what he has will be taken away. 13. This is why I speak to them in parables, because seeing they do not see, and hearing they do not hear, nor do they understand.

14. With them indeed is fulfilled the prophecy of Isaiah which says:

'You shall indeed hear but never understand, and you shall indeed see but never perceive. 15. For this people's heart has grown dull, and their eyes are heavy of hearing, and their eyes they have closed, lest they should perceive with their eyes, and hear with their ears, and understand with their heart, and turn for me to heal them.'

16. But blessed are your eyes, for they see, and your ears, for they hear. 17. Truly, I say to you, many prophets and righteous men longed to see what you see, and did not see it, and to hear what you hear, and did not hear it.

18. "Hear then the parable of the sower. 19. When any one hears the word of the kingdom and does not understand it, the evil one comes and snatches away what is sown in his heart; this is what was sown along the path. 20. As for what was sown on rocky ground, this is he who hears the word and immediately receives it with joy. 21. yet he has no root in himself, but endures for a while, and

when tribulation or persecution arises on account of the word, immediately he falls away. 22. As for what was sown among thorns, this is he who hears the word, but the cares of the world and the delight in riches choke the word, and it proves unfruitful. 23. As for what was sown on good soil, this is he who hears the word and understands it; he indeed bears fruit, and yields, in one case a hundredfold, in another sixty, and in another thirty."

24. Another parable he put before them, saying, "The kingdom of heaven may be compared to a man who sowed good seed in his field; 25. but while men were sleeping, his enemy came and sowed weeds among the wheat, and went away. 26. So when the plants came up and bore grain, then the weeds appeared also. 27. And the servants of the householder came and said to him, Sir, did you not sow good seed in your field? How then has it weeds? 28. He said to them, 'An enemy has done this.' The servants said to him, 'Then do you want us to go and gather them?' 29. But he said, 'No; lest in gathering the weeds you root up the wheat along with them. 30. Let both grow together until the harvest; and at harvest time I will tell the reapers, Gather the weeds first and bind them in bundles to be burned, but gather the wheat into my barn.'"

31. Another parable he put before them, saying, "The kingdom of heaven is like a grain of mustard seed which a man took and sowed in his field; 32. it is the smallest of all seeds, but when it has grown it is the greatest of shrubs and becomes a tree, so that the birds of the air come and make nests in its branches."

33. He told them another parable. "The kingdom of heaven is like leaven which a woman took and hid in three measures of meal, till it was all leavened."

34. All this Jesus said to the crowds in parables; indeed

he said nothing to them without a parable. 35. This was to fulfil what was spoken by the prophet:
"I will open my mouth in parables, I will utter what has been hidden since the foundation of the world."

It is sufficiently clear that the Sower, the purpose of parables, and the Explanation of the Sower (13:3-23) come from a source similar to that of Mark. The editorial phrase, "Another parable he put before them," repeated three times (vv. 24a, 31a, 33a) is the evangelist's way of stringing together the *parables of the Weed, the Mustard Seed* and *the Leaven.*

In *the parable of the Sower,* Matthew consistently uses the plural of seed, thus connoting plenty, and he seems to identify 'the sower' with Jesus. He uses the parable to recapitulate chs. 11-12, and to validate the denunciation and blessing in 13:10-17. The twin accent on failure and success makes this a parable of contrast. The stress is on v. 8a: the word is continuously manifest in the lives of those who respond. The function of the parable in this context is apologetic and paraenctic: it prepares the way for the next passage, which contrasts the Jews and the disciples.

The evangelist's object in compiling the excursus 13: 10-17 is to create a passage in which the disciples (or Church) are placed in strong contraposition to the Jews: disciples and Jews are divided into two estranged camps. Matthew casts the disciples in a favorable light: they are recipients of a special revelation, and are the enlightened

followers of Jesus. They are not only capable of understanding the parables but also do in fact understand them.
We may observe the striking contrast between the per-
plexed attitude of the disciples in Mk 4:10 who "asked
him concerning the parables," and their confident bearing
in Mt 13:10 where they wish to know only: "Why do you
speak to *them* in parables?" For Mark the *unexplained*
parable is as much a riddle to the disciples as to the crowd.
Therefore, Jesus interprets also for the disciples (cf. 4:34)
—who, in fact, as Mark is at pains to underline, fail to understand. Throughout his whole Gospel, by contrast, Matthew endows the disciples with an insight before Easter
which in the other Gospels they do not attain until after
Easter. Therefore, the "disciples" in Mt become the repre-
sentatives of the early Christians.

Matthew (13:13—'because' (*hoti*), and not *hina,* "in
order that" Mk 4:12)—does not say that the parable is
enigmatic in itself but he does stress that in order to comprehend it one must have received from God the capacity
to grasp revelation (vv. 11, 16f). The parable is a riddle
only to the crowds; the disciples, precisely because they are
disciples, are made recipients of divine insight. Thus, they
comprehend the parables of Jesus as a matter of course,
and there is no trace of the rebuke of Mk 4:13. Rather, in
vv. 16f, the disciples are shown to be of privileged status
because of the unique time they live in, the divine revelation imparted to them, and the glorious promise given
them. This is the joyous side of the message.

The somber side is that the Jews are a people under

56

judgment. Matthew has Jesus speak to them in parables because they are blind, deaf, without understanding. This supports the circumstances of the context that they have already proved themselves hardened to the Word. *Now* he *begins* to speak in parables. "In vv. 10-13, the following argument emerges. Because the Jews have rejected the Word of proclamation and consequently demonstrate that they are an obdurate people (v. 13b), God has resolved not to impart to them the secrets of the Kingdom (v. 11). In fact, the Jews have now become a people under judgment (v. 12). In recognition of this, Jesus now addresses them only in parables, i.e. in speech they cannot understand (vv. 10-13)."[3]

Like the preceding passage, the interpretation of the Sower (vv. 18-23) is addressed to the disciples (Church), and not to the Jews or crowds. It expands the topic of "hearing and understanding" (v. 13) and draws the attention of the disciples to moral problems. Then, in v. 24, Jesus turns again to the crowds. The *parable of the Weeds* (vv. 24-30) picks up the argument of vv. 10-17. Grain and weeds grow together: it is Matthew's contemporary situation wherein true Israel and unbelieving Israel are still involved with each other. The Lord gives his directive: "Let both grow together until the harvest" (v. 30). The Church is not to pronounce judgment on unbelieving Israel: the Church's mandate lies in the realm of mission, not of judgment.

The twin parables of Mustard Seed and Leaven are a further link in the polemic against the Jews. Both are

57

parables of contrast. The culmination is most obvious in v. 32: "it becomes a tree, so that the birds of the air come and make nests in its branches." God is at work to establish his final kingdom. Matthew's intention is twofold. It is apologetic: contrary to Jewish belief Jesus tells the Jews that the Kingdom *has* come in his person, though, because of its humble beginnings, not as they had expected it. It is paraenetic: the Lord fortifies the Christians of Matthew's church in their conviction that they *are* the eschatological community.

The words of Jesus' use of parables (vv. 34f) conclude the first half of Matthew's parable discourse. It reiterates the division between Jesus (the disciples and Church) and the Jews. It anchors Jesus' use of parables in salvation history: the discourse in parables is the fulfillment of prophecy. Jesus' thereby testifies to his messiahship and the claim of his Church in his regard is vindicated.

Part II. 13:36-52

36. Then he left the crowds and went into the house. And his disciples came to him, saying, "Explain to us the parable of the weeds in the field." 37. He answered, "He who sows the good seed is the Son of man; 38. the field is the world, and the good seed means the sons of the kingdom; the weeds are the sons of the evil one. 39. and the enemy who sowed them is the devil; the harvest is the close of the age, and the reapers are angels. 40. Just as the weeds are gathered and burned with fire, so will it be at the close of the age. 41. The Son of man will send his angels, and they will gather out of his kingdom all causes of sin and all evil-doers, 42. and throw them into the furnace of fire; there

men will weep and gnash their teeth. 43. Then the right-eous will shine like the sun in the kingdom of their Father. He who has ears to hear, let him hear."

44. "The kingdom of heaven is like treasure hidden in a field, which a man found and covered up; then in his joy he goes and sells all that he has and buys that field."

45. "Again, the kingdom of heaven is like a merchant in search of fine Pearls, 46. who, on finding one pearl of great value, went and sold all that he had and bought it."

47. "Again, the kingdom of heaven is like a net which was thrown into the sea and gathered fish of every kind; 48. when it was full men drew it ashore and sat down and sorted the good into vessels but threw away the bad. 49. So it will be at the close of the age. The angels will come out and separate the evil from the righteous, 50. and throw them into the furnace of fire; there men will weep and gnash their teeth."

51. "Have you understood all this?" They said to him, "Yes." 52. And he said to them, "Therefore every scribe who has been trained for the kingdom of heaven is like a householder who brings out of his treasure what is new and what is old."

"Then he left the crowds and went into the house..." (v. 36). It is a major change of setting. The second half of the parable discourse is directed solely to disciples (Church). Therefore, Matthew chooses for Jesus the privacy of the house. He thus construes 13:36-52 as an ad-dress of Jesus Kyrios, the risen and living Lord, to his Church, and his intention is paraenetic, exhortatory.

In the interpretation of the parable of the Weeds (13:37-43)—a later christian allegorical interpretation which is best examined quite apart from the parable of 13:24-30

—the Lord exhorts the Christians of Matthew's community to be sons of the Kingdom who do God's will. Here Matthew's ethical concern is aided by apocalyptic imagery. This shows how the evangelist regards eschatology as bound up with ethics; that is to say, the Coming Age exerts a pressure which works itself out in the practical life of Christians. (So, the old style hell-fire mission sermon was meant to have a salutary effect on the daily lives of the hearers.) Doing the will of God is not easy. The Christians have "found" the Kingdom: they must stand by their find, at the price of total commitment (the parables of the Treasure and the Pearl). This situation is one marked by urgency—not even the Church itself will be saved from the great Assize. Therefore Christians must continue to do God's will if they are to escape the fate awaiting the godless (parable of the Net, 13:47-50). The question is, do the members of the community understand this? (v. 51). *Understanding* involves knowing the will of God and doing it with single-hearted devotion. As a householder brings out of his storeroom things new and old, so the disciple, in that he knows and does God's will, draws from his heart the revelation God has imparted to him through Jesus, the Lord.

The Jews

Not only in chapter 13, but throughout his Gospel, Matthew evinces a special interest in the role and fate of Israel in history. But, he also feels that there is a single people of God in *both* Testaments which equals the true Israel. God exercises his Lordship in an uninterrupted saving pattern in the two covenants. One should speak, then, not of an old/new Israel but of a false/true people, a people related less to chronology and nationality than to concurrence with God's will. Matthew exposes one aspect of this in describing Israel under judgment. This is especially evident in *the parable of the Wicked Tenants* (21:33-43), in which the Kingdom is to be given to another people of God, a new messianic community in place of the unbelieving Jews. So, too, the obduracy of Israel is not a consequence of Jesus' teaching but a prior fact which necessitated preaching in parables (ch. 13).

The punishment of Israel was known in Matthew's milieu by the destruction of Jerusalem and the Temple. His community saw the ruined city as God's judgment on an unbelieving Israel who had rejected Jesus. The end of *the parable of the Wedding Feast* in 22:7 refers to this punishment in A.D. 70. One could contrast Paul and Matthew. For Paul, God's rejection of Israel was only temporary, although her refusal to accept her Messiah had opened salvation to the Gentiles (Rm 9-11). For Matthew, the rejection was definitive and Israel had no further role to play in salvation history. The different viewpoints are due to different historical circumstances. Paul, apostle to the Gentiles, writing before A.D. 70, could still nourish some hope in the matter of the messianic destiny of his brethren. Matthew, for whom a main subject of concern was the mission of Israel, saw no reason to entertain such hopes. For, he had experienced the hostile reaction to the gospel and had come to interpret the destruction of Jerusalem (already long past) as a sign of divine rejection. Yet he is not really anti-Semitic. His work reflects an historical situation of conflict. For him, simply, the Church as the true Israel is already the place of God's reign, while Israel is dispossessed because she has been unfaithful to her vocation.

Inevitably, there is a tension in any attitude of the Christian Church to Israel. It is present not only in Matthew, but in Paul and in Revelation. In Rm 9-11 Paul does argue that in God's plan the Jewish people, the chosen people, will come to Christ and so finally win its true destiny. Yet, he can also declare: "It is not the children of the flesh who are the children of God, but the children of the promise are reckoned as descendants [of Abraham]" (Rm 9:8; cf. 2:28f; Gal 6:15). The Gentiles now inherit the promise and are become the true people of God. In the letter to Smyrna (Rv 2:8-11) there is reference to "those who say that they are Jews and are not, but are a synagogue of Satan" (v. 9). Despite their claim, these are not really Jews; Christians alone are the true Israel. But the Jews are not thereby neglected. The Christians of Philadelphia receive the promise of the conversion of the Jewish opposition in that city: "Behold, I will make those of the synagogue of Satan who say that they are Jews and are not, but lie—behold, I will make them come and bow down before you, and learn that I have loved you" (3:9). John has turned prophetic declarations on the homage of the Gentiles to Israel (cf. Is 60:14; 43:4) into a promise of the homage of Jews to this small and weak, but loyal, church.

This complex situation is reflected in Matthew. The good news was addressed to Israel, too, and there were many Jewish converts. But always there remained the hostility of official Judaism.

The Parables Today

Matthew's procedure in his chapter 13 is a prime example of the existential understanding of parables. He is not at all concerned to present a Jesus of the past—the historical Jesus—preaching to the crowds and teaching the disciples in Galilee. The evangelist is writing for his community, most of whom had never known Jesus "in the flesh" (cf. 2 Cor 5:16). But for him, as for them, the Lord is still present. His words still ring out, with immediate relevancy, to those later hearers of his message. The situation of contrast is not an object lesson for the community. The characters, all of them, are contemporary: the living Lord, the Church, the Israel that has missed its way. These parables are not an echo from the past; they are the vibrant words of one who lives (cf. Rv 1:18).

Obviously, this process of appropriating and applying the parables of Jesus did not end with Matthew, but has been carried out in every generation since. "Today, too, it is being carried out: by the preacher who would find in the parables of Jesus a message for the present-day people of God. Like Matthew, the preacher adapts these parables to meet the needs of a new and vastly changed situation. Like Matthew, the preacher proclaims them in the same confidence that through his exposition of them Jesus Kyrios,

63

residing in the midst of the Christian assembly, will once again speak to his followers, instructing, exhorting, and admonishing them. Thus, for the preacher and his congregation as for Matthew and his congregation, the parables of Jesus are a living tradition, for through them Jesus Kyrios brings men face to face with that total grace and that total demand that are part and parcel of the Kingdom of Heaven. Consequently, today, too, even as at the time of Matthew, the parables of Jesus can be seen to be an instrument of God for raising up 'sons of the Kingdom': people who, as Matthew would put it, discover the joy of knowing and doing the will of God."[4]

(1) In this chapter I am entirely indebted to the careful and detailed study of J.D. Kingsbury, *The Parables of Jesus in Matthew 13* (London: S.P.C.K. 1969).
(2) J. D. Kingsbury, op. cit., 136.
(3) J.D. Kingsbury, op. cit., 49.
(4) J.D. Kingsbury, op. cit., 137.

CHAPTER IV

SERVANT PARABLES

What does it signify when a whole group of parables has a servant as their central figure? Is this a pictorial or a metaphorical element? What meaning was given to these parables, first by Jesus and then by the evangelists? For Jesus did narrate a definite group of *Servant Parables.*[1] An examination of the usage of different terms for "servant," "to serve" and "service" in the Old Testament, in late Judaism, and in the New Testament, shows that Jesus was making use of a definite idiom of his milieu. However, he employed the concept of "servant" (both in its secular and religious meanings) in his own way. These parables, as he first spoke them, were neither entirely polemical arguments against Jewish authorities nor entirely instruction for the disciples.

There are parables in which a servant appears but which, because no deeper meaning is attached to him, are not *Servant Parables* proper (e.g. the Weed in the Wheat, the Prodigal Son, the Wedding Feast). To this group, too, belongs *the parable of the Wicked Tenants* in which the *douloi* (servants) have the metaphorical meaning of "the prophets." In *the parable of the Wedding Feast* it is to be noted that, although Jesus himself ultimately does fulfill the role of servant, this is *not* explicit in the parable; the servant calling guests to the feast corresponds to Palestinian circumstances.

The Servant Parables proper are: *the Unmerciful Servant, the Unprofitable Servant; the Doorkeeper, the Watchful Servant, the Servant: Faithful and Unfaithful,* and *the Talents.* The first two stand by themselves as distinct from the others, the eschatological Servant Parables. The latter, as they occur in the Gospels, are parables of the Parousia. But one cannot conclude that Jesus gave them such a meaning, simply because there is no other evidence in his whole proclamation that he had this self-consciousness of the Parousia. Their *Sitz im Leben* is the Christian community which had already come to believe in the risen Lord.

It does not appear that the Servant Parables, on the whole, were spoken in controversy with Jesus' opponents and hence they are not "parables of crisis." They are only that in so far as they have the critical function of calling men to watchfulness. As demanded by Jesus, this preparedness was connected with the coming of the Kingdom of which he had already given signs through the expulsion of demons, healing of the sick, and table-fellowship with sinners. After the Resurrection these parables were applied to the Parousia: the "master" becomes Jesus, the servants of whom vigilance and obedience are required become Christians. In so far as there was already pictorial material in these parables for futuristic thought, the Church applied them to the Parousia.

By using the concept of "servant" Jesus is not at all sanctioning the position of slaves. He is merely borrowing another of the many realities in Palestinian life which he makes part of his message. Also, if we nowadays are offended by the setting of the relationship of God and man in terms of Master and servant—as if this belittled the worth of the individual—we must keep in mind that in Palestine the position of the servant was not a despised one. It was the greatest honor to be dependent on a master, and there was a deeply personal relationship between the master and his house servant—almost as close as father and son. It is this concept, which is a firm part of Jesus' proclamation, that can help us to set aright some of the mistaken notions of modern man through the following truth: "namely, that there is no autonomy of man in the presence of God; rather, man in his existence, from first to last, is beholden to God, and the relationship of man to God is a personal one."[2] Finally, both the original Servant Parables and their interpretation by the early Church and in the various synoptic accounts have a single source: the Spirit of Jesus Christ.

The Unmerciful Servant, Mt 18:23-35

23. "Therefore the kingdom of heaven may be compared to a king who wished to settle accounts with his servants. 24. When he began the reckoning, one was brought to him who owed him ten thousand talents; 25. and as he could not pay, his lord ordered him to be sold, and his wife and children and all that he had, and payment to be made. 26. So the servant fell on his knees, imploring him, 'Lord, have

patience with me, and I will pay you everything.' And out of pity for him the lord of that servant released him and forgave him the debt.

28. But that same servant, as he went out, came upon one of his fellow servants who owed him a hundred denarii; and seizing him by the throat he said, 'Pay what you owe.' 29. So his fellow servant fell down and besought him, 'Have patience with me, and I will pay you.' 30. He refused and went and put him in prison till he should pay the debt.

31. When his fellow servants saw what had taken place, they were greatly distressed, and they went and reported to their lord all that had taken place. 32. Then his lord summoned him and said to him, 'You wicked servant! I forgave you all that debt because you besought me; 33. and should not you have had mercy on your fellow servant, as I had mercy on you?' 34. And in anger his lord delivered him to the jailers, till he should pay all his debt.

35. So also my heavenly Father will do to every one of you, if you do not forgive your brother from your heart."

The king's "servant" is, obviously, the governor of a province, responsible for its revenue. But, in fact, no actual situation is in view. The sum involved, about $9,000,000, is deliberately presented as a fantastic debt, impossible of payment. More remarkable still is the lord's cancellation of the whole immense debt; he is moved to pity by the hopeless plea of an official who had proved himself not only wholly incompetent but (we should understand) criminally remiss in his lord's service. Here stands no human master; here is the loving Father. God and the sinner are face to

face and the sinner finds not accusation but forgiveness—
divine forgiveness which passes understanding. And it is
in the context of this limitless mercy that the subsequent
action of the servant is so utterly reprehensible.

Going out from his master's presence, a free man, re-
lieved of an impossible debt, the servant met a minor
official who owed him a relatively trifling sum—about $15.
The same plea as before is heard: "Have patience with me
and I will pay you"—the same plea with a world of difference. The first time we heard it, it was a desperate plea,
incapable of fulfillment. But now it is reasonable—this debt
can be paid off. And yet, this time, it meets with cold indifference. There is no mercy in the heart of one who had
been shown such mercy. It is a shocking state of affairs
which the generous lord cannot tolerate.

The *parable of the Unmerciful Servant* is rooted in
many other sayings of Jesus which express the same message, as, for example, the petition for forgiveness in the
Lord's Prayer (Mt 6:12), where Jesus teaches us to ask
for pardon, as we ourselves are ready to forgive. For, one
who has received God's forgiveness should be himself
forgiving. However, the motive for showing mercy cannot
be in any abstract or distant God, but in this God who is
present in the person of Jesus. Jesus' entire life demonstrates the teaching of mercy which he brings out in the
parable: he took flesh upon himself, he suffered with man,
he invited sinners to table-fellowship and promised them
forgiveness, and he died for them—and for all of us. This

69

parable is far more than a "communication of an abstract truth, more than the teaching of a sage; it is itself the presence here and now of the hour of divine compassion, the beginning of divine salvation."[3] And it is to be noted that human forgiveness is neither the cause nor the condition nor the measure of God's forgiveness of men: "I forgave you all that debt. . . and should not you have had mercy on your fellow servant, as I had mercy on you?" (vv. 33f)

The Parable in Matthew

This last point is rather obscured in Matthew's setting. Matthew has the parable by way of a further commentary on Jesus' reply to Peter's query: "Lord, how often shall my brother sin against me, and I forgive him? As many as seven time?" Jesus said to him, "I do not say to you seven times, but seventy times seven" (18:21f). The parable does indeed give the reason for the unquestioning readiness to forgive. So far so good. But then the evangelist makes an editorial comment, as he does also in 6:14f. "So also my heavenly Father will do to every one of you, if you do not forgive your brother from your heart" (18:35)—"For if you forgive men their trespasses, your heavenly Father also will forgive you; but if you do not forgive men their trespasses, neither will your Father forgive your trespasses" (6:14f). Here, as elsewhere, Matthew is preoccupied with his community, composed of thoroughly human men and women. He sees it as a ship beaten by the waves (8:23-27). He knows that, like the disciples in the gospel, his community has but "little faith." So he multiplies his warnings. This warning in 18:35 is all the more impressive because, coming at the close of his community discourse (ch. 18) it is addressed specifically to the leaders of the community. But the condition put on God's forgiveness is a reflection of Matthew's pastoral concern—it is not the thought of Jesus who stresses the unconditional forgiveness of God. Already we find the Church, in some sort, seeking to put limits to God's mercy—a tendency that, unhappily, was to sharpen in later centuries.

The Unprofitable Servant, Lk 17:7-10

7. "Will any one of you, who has a servant plowing or keeping sheep, say to him when he has come in from the field, 'Come at once and sit down at table?' 8. Will he not rather say to him, 'Prepare supper for me, and gird yourself and serve me, till I eat and drink; and afterward you shall eat and drink?' 9. Does he thank the servant because he did what was commanded? 10. So you also, when you have done all that is commanded you, say, 'We are unworthy servants; we have only done what was our duty.'"

The parable of the Unprofitable Servant is one which would have shocked Jesus' hearers—not through the use of the term *doulos,* but through the manner in which this servanthood is to be lived before God. The picture he has painted is starkly clear. A slave has no claim on his master —neither wages nor thanks—quite independently of how much he may have done for his master. His service is utterly taken for granted. The application of the parable (v.

10) strikes at the very roots of the ethical attitude of contemporary Judaism, a system dominated by the notion of merit. In the Jewish religious consciousness, God "owed" man salvation in view of the just man's fidelity to the Law. But Jesus sets man in *direct* relationship to God, that is, without the law intervening. He establishes man as a *doulos* over against God, standing in obedience to the personal and acknowledged sovereignty of God. There is no doubt that the parable belongs to Jesus' criticism of the theology of his contemporaries: he pronounces a radically negative verdict on the idea of reward. What he does acknowledge is something quite different: the reality of the divine recompense. God's sheer goodness.[4]

The Parable in Luke

Luke begins chapter 17 with the phrase, "He also said to his disciples," but then, in v. 5, the *apostles* ask for an increase in faith, and the parable would seem to be addressed to them. It would appear, then, that Luke has especially in mind the missioners or itinerant preachers of the Gospel. They are reminded of the attitude they ought to have: the consciousness of being slaves who serve their Lord without any claim on a reward. This attitude must inevitably, too, color their relationship to those whom they serve in the Lord's service. But the lesson remains a general one. All disciples, God's slaves, have no claim to reward for doing what God expects of them; they must humbly acknowledge that they are only poor servants.

72

THE ESCHATOLOGICAL SERVANT PARABLES:

The Doorkeeper, Mk 13:33-37

33."Take heed, watch; for you do not know when the time will come. 34. It is like a man going on a journey, when he leaves home and puts his servants in charge, each with his work, and commands the doorkeeper to be on the watch. 35. Watch therefore—for you do not know when the master of the house will come, in the evening, or at midnight, or at cockcrow, or in the morning—36. lest he come suddenly and find you asleep.
37. And what I say to you I say to all: Watch."

The exhortation of v. 33 is Mark's own introduction to the parable. "Take heed" (vv. 5, 9, 23) is the keynote of the farewell discourse of chapter 13 which concludes the narrative of the ministry of Jesus and, in view of his departure from this world, prepares the disciples for events yet to come. "Watch" means "do not permit yourselves to fall asleep!" "Time" (cf. 1:15) is the appointed time fixed in the ordered divine plan. In its context the "time" refers to the unknown "day or hour" of v. 32: "But of that day or of that hour no one knows, not even the angels in heaven, nor the Son, but only the Father." The call to watchfulness in v. 33 brings out the exhortation latent in v. 32. The insertion of v. 33 may well have been suggested by v. 35 of the parable, but it admirably suits Mark s outlook and purpose here.

The Parable

The parable, as Mark found it, had already gone through

a process of reshaping. It certainly resembles the Watching Servants of Lk 12:35-38—indeed, both should be regarded as widely variant forms of the same parable. From Mk 13: 33-36 we may strip away "going on a journey" (34a) and "puts his servants in charge, each with his work" as being out of place in the parable of the Doorkeeper. "We are left with a core which consists of the parable of the Doorkeeper, who had received the command to keep watch (Mk 13: 34b) and to open immediately as soon as his master, on his return from the banquet, should knock (Lk 12:36). It would be well for him if his master should find him watching, at whatever watch of the night he might return (Lk 12:37a, 38; Mk 13:35f)."[5]

The Parable in the Proclamation of Jesus

"It is like a man who leaves home and commands the door-keeper to be on the watch. Watch therefore, for you do not know when the master of the house will come, in the evening, or at midnight, or at cockcrow, or in the morning, lest he come suddenly and find you asleep."

In the proclamation of Jesus the point of the parable concerns that task of the doorkeeper which is connected especially with the absence of his master. It consists in awaiting the arrival of the master and in a readiness to serve him. While his return lies in the *future*, it pre-supposes an act of waiting—a watchfulness—in the present. The doorkeeper must watch *now* in order to be ready when that now coincides with the future moment of arrival. What is this future event? Jesus had proclaimed: "The time is fulfilled, and the kingdom of God is at hand" (1:15). In this parable he calls on men to be ready for its final coming in power. But when that moment is to be can neither be forecast nor reckoned. Watchfulness at all times is the only sensible attitude, indeed the needful attitude.

The Parable in the Tradition

We have noted that the evangelist gave v. 33 its form and prefaced it to the parable; v. 37 is wholly his. The substance of the parable itself (vv. 34-36) he took from the tradition where, already, it was related to a changed situation. The main sentence of v. 35: "Watch therefore ... lest he come suddenly and find you asleep" is the application of the parable. Significantly, it is "the master of the house" who will come—not the "man" of v. 34: it is Christ himself. Vivid expectation of the coming of its Lord was characteristic of the early Church (cf. 1 Th 5:6; 1 Cor 16:22; Rm 13:11; Rv 22:20; also Mt 24:42; Lk 12:40). So, the parable is now understood in christological terms and has been allegorized. Christ is the departing Lord, the Parousia will mark his return, the doorkeeper represents the waiting disciples the community of believers, the divisions of the night are a symbol for the lapse of time before the second advent. "The various implausibilities of the parable are explained if we realize that it envisages a situation something like that of 2 Th; the early Christians very conscious that their Lord is 'away' (v. 34)—perhaps for longer then they had expected (cf. Lk 19:11f)—are warned to be constantly on the watch for his return, but not in any excited or impatient spirit such as would prevent them from applying themselves to the 'service' (v. 34) which has been assigned to each (cf. 2 Th 3:6-13)."[6]

The Parable in Mark

Mark's most significant expansion of the application of the parable is in his phrase, "and puts his servants in charge [literally, 'gives them authority (*exousia*)'], each with his work" (v. 34). *Exousia* is a weighty term in Mark's vocabulary. In 1:22, 27; 2:10; 11:28, 28, 33 it is the authority of Jesus with which he teaches and acts; in 3:15 and 6:7 it is the authority of the twelve, given to them by Jesus. It is because they have *received* authority from Jesus that their only greatness lies in *service* (9:35; 10:44). For Mark, an apostle is a *doulos*—and nevertheless has *exousia*. But Mark is looking, not to the past, but to the present. The authority, given by Jesus to the Twelve, is operative in the evangelist's community. And he looks, not only to the leaders, but beyond them to the whole community: "What I say to you, I say to *all*" (v 36).

Then there is the place of the parable in Mark's Farewell Discourse. The summit of the discourse is reached in 13:26—the Son of Man will come on the clouds of heaven. Mark knows that in and through Jesus' proclamation the Kingdom of God has drawn near (1:15). He was aware that Jesus had spoken of the Kingdom coming in the fullness of power within the span of his own generation (9:1). But now the Christian community needs to have an explanation of why a long interval has elapsed despite Jesus' assurance of the imminence of that coming. Mark had already, in v. 32, given the basic answer: despite the nearness of the coming, the day and hour are known to God alone. The detailing of the night-watches in v. 35 acknowledges the delay and stresses that waiting means watchfulness at every hour. The opening "Take heed" (v. 5) and the final "Watch" (v. 37) emphasize that Mark's real interest in this passage is centered in the exhortation; and his lesson is for all Christians without exception: "I say to *all*." The repeated call to watchfulness indicates how he wanted, not only the parable, but the whole discourse to be understood: not as a guide in calculating a dead-line, but as an invitation and a warning, to live one's life at each moment in preparedness for the meeting with Christ.

The Waiting Servants, Lk 12:35-38

35. "Let your loins be girded and your lamps burning, 36. and like men who are waiting for their master to come home from the marriage feast, so that they may open to him at once when he comes and knocks. 37. Blessed are those servants whom the master finds awake when he comes; truly, I say to you, he will gird himself and have them sit at table, and he will come and serve them. 38. If he comes in the second watch, or in the third, and finds them so, blessed are those servants!"

We have already assumed that the parables of Mark 13:34-36 and Luke 12:36:38, despite notable differences in detail, in their present shape, both go back to a common form. In the Lucan text we may immediately set aside v.

37b, which does not fit the parable precisely as parable. We should accept, too, that the phrase, "to come home from the marriage feast" is an allegorical addition; in the parable, *whence* the master comes is irrelevant. The phrase, "when he comes and knocks" (v. 36) recalls, particularly, the *parable of the Doorkeeper* (who would answer his master's knock) and suggests that the original parable of Jesus is most closely represented in Mark. However, it is likely that Luke's source already spoke of *servants* who waited their master; and the parable, as he had first known it, would have run something like this:

"Be like men who are waiting for their master to come home, so that they may open to him at once when he comes and knocks. Blessed are those servants whom the master finds awake when he comes. If he comes in the second watch, or in the third, and finds them so, blessed are those servants."

The Parable in Luke

The short v. 35 is Luke's introduction to the series of parables (vv. 36-48)—on watchfulness and faithfulness— an exhortation to constant vigilance. The skirts of the long outer garment were tucked into the cincture for freedom of movement; the lamp must be ready and lighted—the ancient oil lamp cannot be lighted by pressing a switch! The servants are expected to sit up for their master who is returning from a wedding. This last detail has all the signs of allegorical development—a reference to the messianic banquet—once the parable had been referred to the

78

Parousia. At any rate, in v. 37b, Luke has an addition which points to the identity of the master because, unlike any earthly master (cf. 17:7-10), he himself will serve the faithful servants. Two texts spring to mind: "I am in the midst of you as he that serves" (22:27) and "I, the Lord and the Master, have washed your feet" (Jn 13:14). This "Master" is manifestly the Lord who, at his coming, welcomes his faithful servants to the Messianic Feast. And now, the "Blessed" of vv. 37 and 38 takes on the sound of eschatological judgment. One might add that the knocking and the opening of v. 36 evokes Rv 3:20—"Behold, I stand at the door and knock; if any one hears my voice and opens the door, I will come in to him and eat with him, and he with me." The true disciple will hear the voice of the Master who is his friend.

From 12:22 onward Jesus had been speaking to his disciples (cf. v. 32); it is to them that the *parable of the Waiting Servants* is addressed, one of his frequent warnings to vigilance. The coming of the Son of Man will be unexpected and watchfulness must characterize the attitude of the disciples who wait for his return. Furthermore, in connection with his solution of the problem of the expectation of an imminent Parousia, our parable stands as a proof for Luke and his community that Jesus himself had indicated an interval before his return.

The Servant: Faithful or Unfaithful. Mt 24:45-51;

Lk 12:42-46, 47f

45. "Who then is the faithful and wise servant, whom his

master has set over his household, to give them their food at the proper time? 46. Blessed is that servant whom his master when he comes will find so doing. 47. Truly, I say to you, he will set him over all his possessions.

48. But if that wicked servant says to himself, 'My master is delayed,' 49. and begins to beat his fellow servants, and eats and drinks with the drunken, 50. the master of that servant will come on a day when he does not expect him and at an hour he does not know, 51. and will cut him in pieces, and put him with the hypocrites; there men will weep and gnash their teeth."

Both this an the Lucan version of the parable come from a Q-form of the text;[7] on the whole, the Matthaean text-form is closer than the Lucan to the form of the text in Q.

The Parable in Q

The positive part of the parable (Mt 24:45-47) tells of a servant whom his master had placed in a position of trust. If he proves trustworthy he will be promoted to a position of much higher dignity: steward of all his master's possessions. The negative part (Mt 24:48-51) tells what will happen if the servant should fail in his trust, neglecting his duties and casting the household into disorder: the master, coming unexpectedly, will punish him. It would seem that the qualifications *faithful and wise servant* (v. 45) and *wicked* servant (v. 48) as well as the phrase "and put him with the hypocrites" are typical allegorical additions to the original text. Then, too, though the detail that the master "is delayed" (v. 48) is a feature of the story, at the time of the formation of Q, a time marked by intense expectation of the coming of the glorified Lord, the term was naturally understood in an eschatological sense. These observations are supported by the fact that already in Q the parable stands in a line of eschatological parables which urge watchfulness in view of the Parousia of Christ (Lk 12:35-38; Lk 12:39f; Mt 24:43f).

In Q, then, the servant is the Christian. The fact of being faithful and wise, or wicked, indicates his consciousness or unawareness of the eschatological situation. The coming of the Lord is the Parousia. Fidelity meets with eternal recompense. The confrontation of the wicked servant with the master is Judgment. The long absence of the master marks the delay of the Parousia; the suddenness of its coming is seen in his unexpected return. The assigning of the wicked servant among the unfaithful is God's final punishment.

The Parable in the Proclamation of Jesus

When we have stripped away the few additional details we have noted in vv. 45, 48 and 51 (and left aside the Matthaean addition "there men will weep and gnash their teeth," v. 51), we are left with a pure parable which must stand very close to the form given it by Jesus himself. It is obviously like the parable of Mk 13:33-37; Lk 12:35-38, but has another thrust. There the emphasis was on watchfulness and the arrival of the master; here it is on the faithful carrying out of a task (or the neglect of it) *during* the absence of the master. His coming is not the goal; it is rather the testing-time, the moment of vindication of or judgment on past conduct.

However, its place in the proclamation of Jesus is the same as that of the Doorkeeper and the Waiting Servants: it belongs to his preaching on the imminence of the Kingdom. Where the doorkeeper was called upon to be continually on watch, the servant in our parable is summoned to abiding faithfulness. The establishment of the servant in a position of authority and his special commission to feed and care for the members of the household serve the exposition: the servant is in a situation wherein he must render an account to his master. The details are meant to make his accountability especially evident.

The return of the master is a crucial factor. At that moment it will emerge whether the conduct of the servant has been faithful service or culpable neglect. Because that return happens suddenly and unexpectedly, the attitude of fidelity to an entrusted task becomes an attitude of abiding readiness. The parable aims at this. It is less an admonishment to faithful service than a call to preparedness. This preparedness is in view of the coming of the Kingdom. Already the hearers of Jesus had been made aware of its inbreak; they were witnesses of his deeds of power, especially his exorcisms and healings. Now Jesus refers to its final coming in its fullness. Our parable fits the pattern of Jesus' preaching of the Kingdom also under its twofold aspect of promise of salvation and proclamation of disaster. Jesus consistently promises salvation and entry into the Kingdom to one who opens himself to the summons of his word and he threatens with exclusion from the Kingdom one who hesitates to listen to his call to conversion. We should, then, understand this parable, in Jesus' intention, as both promise and warning in view of the final coming of the Kingdom.

The Parable in Matthew

Matthew has emphasized the eschatological aspect of the parable already present in Q. He has done so, in the first place, by the arrangement of its context. In his chapter 24, after he had insisted that the moment of the return of the Son of Man is known to God (v. 36) he adds, from Q, three short parables which stress the unexpectedness, the suddenness of the Parousia and which call to watchfulness and readiness: the Flood (vv. 37-39), One Taken One Left (vv. 40f), the Burglar (v. 43). These short, picturesque parables direct the glance on the sudden, unexpected coming of the Lord. Then follow three further parables: the Servant: Faithful or Unfaithful (vv. 45-51), the Ten Maidens (25:1-13) and the Talents (25:14-30). In contrast to the others, these are much longer, have in view not only the moment of return but are specially concerned with conduct in the interval and, indeed, suggest a long absence of the Lord. Next, there is Matthew's addition of v. 51b: "there men will weep and gnash their teeth" (cf. 22:13; 25:30). This has no place in the parable proper. Rather, it refers to sanctions after death; the phrase describes the place of the unfaithful, the rejected. The narrative has become an account of Judgment.

PARABLES TOLD BY JESUS

Also present in Matthew is the ecclesial dimension: a glance at the Matthaean community. In place of Luke's "menservants and maidservants" (Lk 12:45) Matthew has "fellow-servants" (v. 49): perhaps a reference to the thoughtless and loveless attitude of members of the community towards their fellow Christians. There are other indications in Matthew that all was not well in his community: *the parable of the Weed in the Wheat* (13:24-30, 36-43), scandals (18:21-35), need of fraternal corrrection (18:15-17), need of mutual forgiveness (18:21-35) and the warning that, before the end, many will fall away and love will grow cold (24:10-12). The parable, then, sounds a note of warning. Some within the community might well see themselves in that wicked servant.

The Parable in Luke (12:42-48)

42. And the Lord said, "Who then is the faithful and wise steward, whom his master will set over his household, to give them their portion of food at the proper time? 43. Blessed is that servant whom his master when he comes will find so doing. 44. Truly I tell you, he will set him over all his possessions.
45. But if that servant says to himself, 'My master is delayed in coming,' and begins to beat the menservants and the maidservants, and to eat and drink and get drunk, 46. the master of that servant will come on a day when he does not expect him and at an hour he does not know, and will cut him in pieces, and put him with the unfaithful.
47. And that servant who knew his master's will, but did not make ready or act according to his will, shall receive a severe beating. 48. But he who did not know, and

84

did what deserved a beating, shall receive a light beating. Every one to whom much is given, of him will much be required; and of him to whom men commit much they will demand the more."

The question of v. 41—"Peter said, 'Lord, are you telling this parable for us or for all?'"—is absent from Matthew and its style betrays the hand of Luke: it refers to the preceding parable of the Waiting Servants (12:36-38). The parable proper (vv. 42-46) deals with the alternative conduct of a servant whom his master would place in charge of his affairs while he himself was absent on a long journey. Especially significant, in v. 42, is the change of "servant" (*doulos*) to "steward" (*oikonomos*) (cf. Mt 24:45). When Luke wrote his gospel, hellenistic Christians saw their leaders as God's stewards (cf. 1 Cor 4:1f; Tt 1:7; 1 P 4:10). They are God's deputies, acting not in their own name but in his. Hence, they are not masters of the community but men dedicated to its service. As stewards, God's stewards, they are more than ever *servants* (cf. Lk 6:39-45; 22:24-27). In Acts 20:17-35 Paul movingly outlines, in personal terms, the quality of community service. For Luke, service is the essence of office in the Church.

The verses 47-48a (not in Matthew) have no more than a loose link with the parable; they introduce the fresh idea that the punishment of disobedience will be in proportion to knowledge of the Master's will. They are likely not from Jesus but constitute a community saying: their casuistic tone is foreign to his preaching. V. 48 stands on its own. The passive and the impersonal forms are in place of the divine name, and the verse might be rendered: "Of every one to whom God has given much will he require much; and of him to whom God has entrusted much will he demand the more." Whatever the provenance and the original meaning of vv. 47f, there is no doubt of their meaning in the Lucan context. The office-holders (the "stewards") are those who know the will of their Lord and have the duty to make it known. If they do not live according to this knowledge they deserve a greater punishment than others. The purpose of these words is to summon those who hold office in the community to faithful and selfless service of their Lord and of the Christians entrusted to their care.

The Talents/The Pounds, Mt 25:14-30; Lk19: 12-27

(Mt 25:14-30). 14. For it will be as when a man going on a journey called his servants and entrusted to them his property; 15. to one he gave five talents, to another two, to another one, to each according to his ability. Then he went away. 16. He who had received the five talents went at once and traded with them; and he made five talents more. 17. So too, he who had the two talents made two talents more. 18. But he who had received the one talent, went and dug in the ground and hid his master's money. 19. Now after a long time the master of those servants came and settled accounts with them. 20. And he who had received the five talents came forward, bringing five talents more, saying, "Master, you delivered to me five talents; here I have made five talents more." 21. His master said to him, "Well done, good and faithful servant; you have been faith-

86

ful over a little, I will set you over much; enter into the joy of your master." 22. And he also who had the two talents came forward, saying, "Master, you delivered to me two talents; here I have made two talents more." 23. His master said to him, "Well done, good and faithful servant; you have been faithful over a little, I will set you over much; enter into the joy of your master." 24. He also who had received the one talent came forward, saying, "Master, I knew you to be a hard man, reaping where you did not sow, and gathering where you did not winnow; 25. so I was afraid, and I went and hid your talent in the ground. Here you have what is yours." 26. But his master answered him, "You wicked and slothful servant! You knew that I reap where I have not sowed, and gather where I have not winnowed? 27. Then you ought to have invested my money with the bankers, and at my coming I should have received what was my own with interest. 28. So take the talent from him, and give it to him who has the ten talents."

29. For to every one who has will more be given, and he will have abundance; but from him who has not, even what he has will be taken away. 30. And cast the worthless servant into the outer darkness; there men will weep and gnash their teeth.

Despite notable differences, the Talents (Matthew) and the Pounds (Luke) are versions of the same parable. However, the last two verses of Matthew's text (vv.29f) are not really part of the parable at all but are designed to widen its application and refer it to the Judgment.

The Parable in the Proclamation of Jesus

We may take it that Mt 25:14-28 represents, sufficiently

closely for our purpose, the parable of Jesus. It is significant that, despite the wide discrepancy in detail, Matthew and Luke agree to a notable extent in their accounts of the last servant. And this is not surprising, for indeed the parable is primarily concerned with the action (rather, the inactivity) of the cautious servant. True, in Mt 25:26, he is called slothful, but this precision is not present in Luke. What is really the matter with him is a paralyzing fear: "I was afraid" (Mt 25:25); "I was afraid of you" (Lk 19:21). And he feared because of his image of his master: "I knew you to be a hard man, reaping where you did not sow, and gathering where you did not winnow" (Mt 25:24). In all the Servant Parables the servant metaphor expresses man's relationship with God. Our parable is not concerned with culpable indolence or inexcusable lack of enterprise; it is concerned with a man who has never really known his master. It is concerned with men whose God is a hard, severe Lord, a tyrant. Jesus wants to show that obedience to such a caricature of God is vitiated at its source: men will respond legalistically to such a God.

It is natural to suppose that Jesus has in mind the "righteousness" of the scribes and Pharisees, which Joachim Jeremias has so aptly and so frighteningly characterized as "the piety which separates from God."[8] They are men who "for the sake of their tradition had made void the word of God" (Mt 15:6). They are men who "tithed mint and dill and cummin, and have neglected the weightier matters of the law, justice and mercy and faith" (23:23). They are men "who shut the kingdom of heaven against men; for they neither enter themselves, nor allow those who would enter to go in" (23:13). They are men who "bind heavy burdens, hard to bear, and lay them on men's shoulders; but they themselves will not move them with their finger" (23:4). They are men who were scandalized by a deed of mercy done on the sabbath (cf. Lk 13:14). Such an attitude inevitably affected their idea of God, or as engendered by their image of him: a hard master, reaping where he did not sow, a God not to be loved but to be feared.

C. H. Dodd is surely right in regarding the third servant of our parable as "the type of pious Jew who comes in for such criticism in the Gospels. He seeks personal security in a meticulous observance of the Law... The parable, I suggest, was intended to lead such persons to see their conduct in its true light."[9] They are like the elder son of the parable of the Prodigal Son: their service of God is loveless, because they do not know him as Father.

Is the point of the parable *only* in the dialogue with the third servant, while the others serve as foils to him? Or is their conduct, too, significant for an understanding of the parable? If, like the other Servant Parables, the subject of this also is the Kingdom, then there is a lesson in the conduct of all three. And the Kingdom is like a treasure, like a very costly pearl (Mt 13:44-46); and it is like seed which grows of itself, having within it, implanted there by God, its own principle of growth (Mk 4:26-29). In our parable the capital entrusted to the servants is not only a treasure but also is meant to increase—the master takes for granted that interest will accrue (Mt 25:27). The first two servants understood the nature of the gift—because they understood the nature of the God of the Kingdom. The other understood neither God nor the nature of God's gift. The Kingdom is not something one keeps for oneself.

In the preaching and life of Jesus, the Kingdom is the manifestation of God's goodness, of his fatherly love and mercy. The hallmark of Jesus' preaching of the Kingdom was: "the *poor* have the good news preached to them." Yet when, time and again, Jesus declares emphatically that the salvation he brings is for the poor and that he has come as a Savior of *sinners,* he is not preaching to the poor and to sinners; for them he himself is the sermon that has won them. They receive his gift gladly, like the first servants of the parable. The others, who will not receive him, Jesus strives to bring to look at themselves. They are like the guests who disdainfully declined the invitation to the feast, and then looked with contempt on those who had taken their place (Mt 22:1-10; Lk 14:16-24). They are like the vinedressers who arrogantly insulted their Lord and maltreated his servants. They are those who have already chosen for themselves the best places in the Kingdom, but who are warned that God's assessment of their worth may not quite square with the opinion they have formed of themselves—they may be lucky to be offered even the lowest place (Lk 14:7-11). They are like the third servant of the parable whose legalism had so distorted his vision that he saw God only as a stern and fearsome taskmaster. Such as he cannot understand that message of good news. Again and again Jesus is asked by such as he: "Why do you mix with the godless rabble?" Tirelessly, he replies:

> Because they are sick and need me, because they are truly repentant, and because they feel the gratitude of children forgiven by God. Because, on the other hand, you, with your loveless, self-righteous, disobedient hearts, have rejected the gospel. But, above all, because I know what God is like, so good to the poor, so glad when the lost are found, so overflowing with a father's love for the returning child, so merciful to the despairing, the helpless, and the needy. That is why![10]

The Parable in Matthew

Matthew has set the parable in the last of the five discourses of his Gospel—the eschatological discourse. In that context, it has to do with the second coming of the Son of Man and stands as a warning to the disciples of Christ that at his coming he will take account of the manner in which they had made use of the gifts they had received and of the opportunities that had presented themselves. The eschatological note is very clear in the phrase: "enter into the joy of your master" (vv. 21, 23), for "joy" really stands for "joyous feast"—the Messianic Banquet. And the closing verse, v. 30, patently refers to the Last Judgment. This verse is the evangelist's own composition, containing his characteristic expressions: "cast into the outer darkness" (cf 22:13) and "there men will weep and gnash their teeth" (22:13; 24:51). V. 29 is an isolated saying of Jesus (cf. Mt 13:12; Mk 4:25; Lk 8:18) added to widen the application of the parable. The passive is the "divine passive": "God will give . . . will take away." And the paradoxical second part of it says: From him who has not (profit to show) is taken (withdrawn) even that (capital) which he still has.

Here, too, Matthew has his community, his imperfect community, in mind. At the start, "the disciples came to him privately" (24:3) and the whole discourse is addressed to them. The conduct of the third servant would stand as a warning to some in his church.

The Parable in Luke (19:12-27)

11. As they heard these things, he proceeded to tell them a parable, because he was near to Jerusalem, and because they supposed that the kingdom of God was to appear immediately. 12. He said therefore:
A nobleman went into a far country to receive kingly power and then return. 13. Calling ten of his servants, he gave them ten pounds, and said to them, "Trade with these till I come." 14. But his citizens hated him and sent an embassy after him, saying, "We do not want this man to reign over us." 15. When he returned, having received the kingly power, he commanded these servants, to whom

he had given the money, to be called to him, that he might know what they had gained by the training. 16. The first came before him, saying, "Lord, your pound has made ten pounds more." 17. And he said to him, "Well done, good servant! Because you have been faithful in a very little, you shall have authority over ten cities." 18. And the second came, saying, "Lord, your pound has made five pounds." 19. And he said to him, "and you are to be over five cities." 20. Then another came, saying, "Lord, here is your pound, which I kept laid away in a napkin; 21. for I was afraid of you, because you are a severe man; you take up what you did not lay down, and reap what you did not sow." 22. He said to him, "I will condemn you out of your own mouth, you wicked servant! You knew that I was a severe man, taking up what I did not lay down and reaping what I did not sow? 24. Why then did you not put my money into the bank, and at my coming I should have collected it with interest?" 24. And he said to those who stood by, "Take the pound from him, and give it to him who has the ten pounds." 25. And they said to him, "Lord, he has ten pounds!"

26. "I tell you, that to every one who has will more be given; but from him who has not, even what he has will be taken away. 27. But as for these enemies of mine, who did not want me to reign over them, bring them here and slay them before me."

Woven into the fabric of the Pounds is the story of a nobleman who went abroad to make sure of his right to a throne (v. 12). Though an embassy of his own people tried to forestall him (v. 14) he did return as king; and set about rewarding his supporters (vv. 17, 19) and punishing his enemies. These features recall an episode of 4 B.C. when, on the death of Herod the Great, his son Archelaus went to Rome to be confirmed in his possession of Judas. A deputation of Jews attempted to block his claim but Archelaus won out and, on his return, took a bloody revenge on those who had opposed him. This secondary parable, the Pretender, would have been a warning to the Jews, a parable of judgment.

In Luke the composite parable has taken on marked allegorical traits: the nobleman is Christ who has to leave this world before returning in glory; his own citizens who do not accept him are the Jews (cf. Jn 1:11); the servants are the disciples whom he expects to work with the "capital" he has given them. When he comes to judge there will be a reckoning and the servants will be rewarded according to their deserts. The unbelieving Jews will receive particularly severe punishment; this last point is, of course, the lesson of the Pretender.

In an introductory verse that shows manifest traces of his style (19:11), Luke has told us how he understood this new (composite) parable for, by placing it in the context of the entry into Jerusalem, he related it explicitly to the Parousia. But he does so that the parable may appear as a clear rebuttal of the vivid expectation of many Christians of his time (cf. Ac 1:6f). The parable takes its place among the statements in which Luke has given his solution to the Parousia-problem of the early Church, a solution which is valid to the present day: No matter how long it may be until the Lord returns, what matters for his disciples is to continue in faithful service, making the best use of the gifts the Master has given them.[11]

(1) In this chapter I am much indebted to an important book of Alfons Weiser, *Die Knechtsgleichnisse der Synoptischen Evangelien* (München: Kösel-Verlag 1971). He is the first to have studied the Servant Parables in depth *as a group.*
(2) A. Weiser, op. cit., 275.
(3) A. Weiser, op. cit., 97.
(4) J. Jeremias, *New Testament Theology* I. The Proclamation of Jesus (London: SCM 1971), 147-157.
(5) J. Jeremias, *The Parables of Jesus* (London: SCM 1963[2]), 55.
(6) D.E. Nineham, *Saint Mark* (London: Penguin Books 1963), 361.
(7) "Q" (from the German *Quelle* = "source") is the conventional designation of the hypothetical common source followed by Matthew and Luke for material that is not in Mark. Yet, it is impossible to give a coherent form to this source; it may be described as a common source only with qualifications. It is not difficult to imagine that the rather formless collection of sayings and parables of Jesus would have been freely modified and expanded in different communities. The "common" source of Mt and Lk may well have been two widely diversified forms of original traditions that had stood close together.
(8) J. Jeremias, *New Testament Theology*, 147-151.
(9) C.H. Dodd, *The Parables of the Kingdom* (London: Collins 1961[2]), 112.
(10) J. Jeremias, *The Parables of Jesus*, 146.
(11) A. Weiser, op. cit., 272.

CHAPTER V

THE SOWER

3. "Listen! A sower went out to sow. 4. And as he sowed, some seed fell along the path, and the birds came and devoured it. 5. Other seed fell on rocky ground, where it had not much soil, and immediately it sprang up, since it had no depth of soil; 6. and when the sun rose it was scorched, and since it had no root it withered away. 7. Other seed fell among thorns and the thorns grew up and choked it, and it yielded no grain. 8. And other seeds fell into good soil and brought forth grain, growing up and increasing and yielding thirtyfold and sixtyfold and a hundredfold." 9. And he said, "He who has ears to hear, let him hear."

The text of the parable is notably Semitic and must stand close to an Aramaic original, and the lines of it are very simple and clear. But, because we can no longer be sure of its precise setting in the ministry of Jesus, there is some doubt about its meaning. We shall put forward two main lines of interpretation. The parable's effectiveness lies in its being a precise account of daily activity, cast in the realm of actual experience. "You know how it is. . ."— the many factors a farmer must cope with in sowing, the risks he must take. The parable is true to life because it shows the actual details of Palestinian ploughing and sowing. Structurally, the parable falls into two parts: the first is negative—the grain and seedlings and young plants perish; the second is positive—the rest of the grain flourishes and the yield is striking. "Listen" (v. 3) echoes the "Hear" of Dt 6:4. For Mark the admonition highlights, from the outset, the importance of 'hearing' throughout this narrative (cf. v. 9). It also suggests that parables are meant to provoke thought.

"As he sowed"—the scene is vivid: one can picture the sparrows gathering to peck away at the fallen grain. The situation depicted here (vv. 4-7) is typically Palestinian. In Palestine, sowing comes before ploughing (as with us the seed is scattered before harrowing); hence, it is natural for the farmer to sow apparently helter-skelter as he does. He sows intentionally on the casual path which the villagers have trod through the stubble because it is going to be ploughed up (and the seed ploughed in at the same time). He sows intentionally among the withered thorns, because these, too, are going to be ploughed up. He cannot avoid the rocks that jut through the thin soil. In vv. 5f the withering is due to the same cause which led to rapid growth: the shallowness of the soil which did not permit the plant to form its roots. The thorns grew faster and higher than the wheat and "choked" it—a strong, descriptive word (v. 7).

In vv. 5 and 7 we had "other (seed)" (*allo*) in the singular; in v. 8 it is plural "other (seeds)" (*alla*). Up until now the interest has borne first of all on the quality of the soil which received the seed. But, in v. 8, the interest passes from the soil to the seed. Since the field remains the same, it is the difference in quality in the seed which produces more or less abundant fruit. This shift of emphasis explains the plural *alla;* it is motivated by the mention of different yields, necessitating a distinction between different kinds of grain. The change is editorial. The abundance of the yield is expressed in extravagant terms. The point of the parable is found in this verse: though part of the seed is lost, the rest falls on good soil and the yield is beyond all expectation.

The parable ends (v. 9), as it began, with a solemn call to hear. The saying occurs frequently, in various forms, and with one exception (Rv 13:9) is always an utterance of Jesus (cf. Mk 4:23; Mt 11:15; 13:9; Lk 14:35) or the risen Lord (Rv 2:7, 11, 17, 29; 3:6, 13, 22; 13:9). In the present case, its implication that not everyone is capable of understanding the parable prepares the way for the explanation.

1. The Meaning of the Sower

What is the meaning of the parable of the Sower? A host of differing opinions may be reduced to five.

1) Jesus is portraying himself as the Sower. He is telling of his fortunes in Galilee, the failure and success of his mission in the early days; at this point, the word was received with enthusiasm. This interpretation lends actuality to the parable; but something deeper is needed.

2) The point lies in the *growth,* the processes which each

kind of seed undergoes. It is the story of a farmer's fortunes: despite the inevitable waste and obstacles, he does have an excellent crop. The point is that now is the time to reap. God is at work even amidst the obstacles and oppositions. This gives the reader a deeper understanding when he meets with the Cross and Resurrection.

3) The emphasis lies on attentive hearing. The birds, thorns, rocks and parching sun are more than just stage props. They really are the things which interfere with the *hearing* of the word.

4) The most universally accepted interpretation is the eschatological one—or, at least, this in combination with the idea of reaping here and now. In this view, the emphasis lies on the *crop*, the harvest. This harvest denotes the inbreak of the Kingdom. The very abundance of the yield indicates the eschatological overflowing of divine grace surpassing all human measure. Thus, it is a parable of *contrast*. There is the sowing with the manifold frustration to which a farmer's work is liable; and there is the harvest which gives the picture of a ripening field, a different time altogether. This time is the future coming of the Kingdom. An objection to this interpretation is precisely that, it concerns only the future, whereas surely Jesus would have stressed the present coming of the Kingdom in himself.

5) As an extension of the preceding view, the Sower himself is seen as an Eschatological Personage (he is *ho speirōn,* "he who sows," and the particle "behold"

focuses our attention on him). He sets a whole movement afoot by his sowing (as implied by the aorist
verb, "went out," a single moment). The point of the
parable is the *yield* in respect of different kinds of soil.
The Old Testament background is instructive: God is
to sow a people for himself, Ho 2:23; Jr 31:27; there
is a seeding to be raised up by Yahweh, Zc 6:12f. The
Sowing brings about a new creation. Jesus proclaims
the inbreak of the eschatological era: the Sower
(eschatological personage) meets with the soil (the
eschatological people of God). He seeds it with the
eschatological seed of God; that soil must be good to
receive the seed. This is the living history of Encounter.

Jesus had proclaimed the coming to the Kingdom, with
varying results. Some remained closed to his message: the
"wise and prudent," the scribes who attributed his exorcisms to the power of Beelzebul (Mk 3:22). Others had
heard, but without bringing forth the fruit of conversion,
like the inhabitants of Capernaum and Chorazin (Mt 11:
20-24). But still others have heard and have followed
Jesus. The different reactions correspond to the different
kinds of soil in the fields planted by the sower. Thus, it is
not a parable of growth, and it is not a parable of simple
contrast between sowing and harvest. It is not, properly
speaking, a parable of the Kingdom—if one means by that
a lesson on the manner in which God establishes the
Kingdom—because this would mean leaving in the shade

the intrinsic relationship of seed and soil to the person of the sower.

One thing at least is sure: however one takes it, the Sower expresses the confident assurance of Jesus that his work cannot fail. The seed has been sown; come what may, the yield (and the harvest) will be very great.

2. *The* Sitz im Leben *of the Sower*

While the original setting of the parable is not at all clear, we may envisage two appropriate situations. The first preaching of the gospel has been well received. But, one can equally well already perceive forces of opposition and inertia at work. Against these, the parable says, *faith* must speak its "nevertheless"—the certainty that, despite all the opposition and hinderances suffered by his Word, *nevertheless* God is at work and does bring forth the end he has promised. Jesus' opponents could have objected that too much of his work has been a failure. "True," he says, "but no farmer delays to reap just because he spies bare patches in a field. The harvest too is plentiful; all that is lacking are the laborers to reap it." Or, Jesus' disciples have grown despondent and filled with doubts because of the apparent meagerness of his following, as expressed in the parables of *the Mustard Seed* and *the Leaven*. Here, these doubts take a specific form: Jesus' preaching is apparently so ineffectual; hostility and increasing desertions are abounding. And so, he says to the, "Consider the husbandman. He might well despair; yet he remains unshaken in confidence. How is it that you have no faith" (cf. Mk 4:40). Thus, the parable is

Jesus' encouragement to his faint-hearted disciples. This is significant; for it is understandable that his own confidence should be unshaken. But that he enjoins it also on the disciples shows that they must not only be content to believe the Good News and acknowledge its import; they must also entrust themselves to its power at work already in Jesus' preaching. This parable could belong to the last period of the Galilean ministry when a great part of the people deserted Jesus while a little group of disciples remained faithful.

We must remember that the Sower had a long history before Mark recorded it. Those who transmitted and wrote it down were not historians. They were not concerned with what and how Jesus spoke at one particular moment. Rather, they were concerned with his words because in them they found an answer to their own difficulties and situation. Thus, though the parable's original meaning can no longer be clearly perceived, we can still see how the early Church understood it. For, we shall find that the Explanation of the Sower (4:13-20) represents some sort of effort on the part of Jesus' followers to discern more clearly what the Sower really meant.

3. *The Message of the Sower*

The Sower in the mind of Jesus surely represented part of his call to believe; one can hear it expressing his lament, "O ye of little faith." *Jesus* can see beyond human eyes— beyond what appears so much wasted and profitless seed in a farmer's field. He can see to the harvest. One needs only to compare the numbers of his "little flock" while he was on earth and now. Both the Sower and its Explanation demonstrate that the Kingdom's real triumph is the triumph of Jesus' word over men's hearts. The perspective opened up by the harvest—whether seen as eschatological or here and now—is that of a new world, new possibility.

In a sense, the parable illustrates the fate of every labor, the hopelessness of every work. It is that same timeless cycle of pathos lamented in Qoheleth (2:17b-20, 22f). On the other hand, like the little parable of the "seed growing secretly" in Mark, it relates the rhythm of seedtime and harvest such as is promised by Yahweh in Gn 8:22. This rhythm is not a biological law, but an argument of his creative Goodness. The rhythm of seedtime and harvest is God's prescription and will. It is a parable of the rhythm of the coming Kingdom. One could also say that the Sower is speaking of Adam's field in Gn 3:17f ("Cursed is the ground because of you . . . thorns and thistles it shall bring forth to you; and you shall eat the plants of the field. In the sweat of your face you shall eat bread . . ."). Here is the *real* Palestinian field!

The audience of the parable is faced with the question of Mt 11:2-6—"Are you he who is to come, or do we await another?" It is a radical question in which the eschatological horizon becomes one with the present moment. And Jesus is *still* sowing seeds in men's hearts.

How should one preach the parable of the Sower in the 20th century? The problem is that, in a technological society, people are more familiar with mass production and packets of cellophaned foods than with the routine of a farm worker. Thus, the preacher must first point to the real background, the hand-to-mouth existence of a Palestinian small-holder. He must tell the setting of the story. "Here was this Carpenter of Nazareth . . ."—and all the subsequent feelings that the crowds must have had about him. One must also tell about how the disciples could grow disheartened at his early stage of the ministry. This is why Jesus tells them the story of a farmer undaunted by failure. The disciples listening to the story and hearing the ending in the bumper crop, would have suddenly become aware that it all had a deeper meaning. They would look over the whole history of their people and see how, despite all, God's purpose for Israel had never been defeated.

Those who heard Jesus speak the parable and were not yet committed believers were at least challenged to think more about who this Carpenter could be. Those who were already his followers would have seen his words as a call to faith and hope. Had it not always been so in the annals of God's servants? Although there were setbacks and hostility from ecclesiastics, yet God continued to accomplish his purposes through them. Jesus' followers then took his message with a deeper sense of urgency. They had committed their lives to this Man. Now he was assuring them of their role in the greatest drama of all time. They began to take him at his word because they loved him and trusted him.

However, God works through *ordinary* men and women. This is where the Explanation of the Sower comes into play. We need faith in God—but *he* depends on *us.* We are the soil on which his good seed falls—the seed of his word, the sacraments, the message of his love. But, what kind of soil *are* we?... Few of us will be like that soil which produces the thirty or sixty or hundredfold. But God can still do much with men and women who make even a fivefold return for all they have received from him.[1]

II. An Explanation of the Parable of the Sower. Mk 4:13-20 (Mt 13:18-23;Lk 8:11-15)

13. And he said to them, "Do you not understand this parable? How then will you understand all the parables?" 14. The sower sows the word. 15. And these are the ones along the path, where the word is sown; when they hear, Satan immediately comes and takes away the word which is sown in them. 16. And these in like manner are the ones sown upon rocky ground, who, when they hear the word, immediately receive it with joy; 17. and they have no root in themselves, but endure for a while; then, when tribulation or persecution arises on account of the word, immediately they fall away. 18. And others are the ones sown among thorns; they are those who hear the word. 19. but the cares of the world, and the delight in riches, and the desire for other things, enter in and choke the word, and it proves unfruitful. 20. But those that were sown upon the good soil are the ones who hear the word and accept it and bear fruit, thirtyfold and sixtyfold and a hundred-fold."

Like many of the parables of Jesus, the Sower found a new setting in the life of the early Church; it has become an exhortation to converts to examine themselves and to test the sincerity of their conversion. In order to achieve this purpose, the parable had been allegorized. A study of the vocabulary confirms the impression that the explanation is indeed a later development, a product of the primitive Church. When we look at it squarely it is obvious that the explanation of the Sower is somewhat forced. Two inconsistent lines have been followed: the seed is the word and, at the same time, represents classes of people. This fusion of two concepts is also found in 4 Ezra: the divine word as God's seed (9:31) and men as God's planting (8:41). In the Explanation, the details of the parable, which had been incidental, become symbolical and the emphasis is on the hearers' reception of the word. This fits into the Marcan context with its presentation of two levels of understanding: hearing and perceiving the Word. The explanation suggests that it is Satan who blocks the transition from the first to the second of these two levels through the medium of the allures, cares and tribulations of the world. Thus, the explanation is bound up with the problem of the hearers: nothing in the world seems so surrounded by dangers and obstacles than man's hearing the Word! It is not so much types of men who are described here as men in encounter with the Word. This carries with it the possibility of believing; for believing is not abstract: it is, precisely, the meeting of men with the Word.

The Marcan link-formula, "And he said to them," joins the explanation of the Sower to the evangelist's insertion on the use of parables. V. 13 seems to have been retouched, or redrafted, by Mark in accordance with his motif of the incomprehension of the disciples; from v. 10 it emerges that the unexplained parable is a riddle to the disciples too. We find the same tendency to generalize as in vv. 10f; it is not a question of the interpretation of a parable but of the 'science of parables'. The reproachful tone, too, is characteristic of Mark (cf. 7:18; 8-17-21, 33); we may reasonably regard it as an editorial trait. There is a contradiction, or so it would appear, between vv. 11 and 13: on the one hand it is affirmed that the disciples cannot understand without a special "gift" of God, while in v. 13 they are blamed for their lack of understanding. In fact, both affirmations are aspects of the special theology of Mark, and aspects of the same eschatological reality. The slowness of the disciples to understand only sets in relief the greatness of the revelation that is granted to them. Besides, the disciples, by themselves, cannot come to see the mystery of the Kingdom—Jesus must open their eyes. "Understand"—the Greek make a clear distinction between *oida*, to know by intuition or insight ("Do you not *know* this parable?"), and *ginōskō*, to know by observation or experience ("How then will you *understand* all the parables?"). The tenor of the question would appear to be: if you have failed to understand this parable (the Sower)— about listening and hearing the word (vv. 3, 9)—how are you going to understand the parables in general?

The explanation of the Sower is a commentary which takes up and explains each phrase of the parable. In v. 14

"the Sower" is the sower of the parable and is not further identified. "The word" (*ho logos*), used absolutely, is a technical term for the Gospel, coined, and currently employed by the primitive Church (cf. Ac 6:7; 12:24; Col 1:6, 10; 1 Th 1:6; 1 Tm 1:8; 1 P 2:8; Jm 1:21). In the gospels, however, it is very significant that the absolute use of *ho logos* by Jesus occurs only in the interpretation of the Sower (eight times in Mk, five times in Mt, and three times in Lk). In v. 15 the phrase, "some seed fell along the path" of 4:4 is taken up. Here the interest is on the hearers of the word; the type of soil, "along the paths," is taken to represent a class of hearers. The thieving birds in 4:4 are allegorized; Luke (8:12) explains of Satan: "that they may not believe and be saved."

In vv. 16, 18 and 20 it is *men* who are "sown"; they are now identified with the seed and no longer with the types of soil. The explanation takes up (v. 16) the case of the seed which "fell on rocky ground" (4:5). The enthusiastic joy of the hearers is like the precocious growth of the seedling, and it is equally ephemeral. The use of *hriza*, "roots," meaning internal stability (cf. Col 2:7; Ep 3:17), and the term *proskairos*, "for a while" (cf. 2 Cor 4:18; Heb 11:25) do not occur elsewhere in the synoptics. The inevitable awkwardness remains: the seed is not the word (v. 14) and the hearers of the word.

From v. 17b onward the experiences of the early Christian community are reflected, beginning with troubles and persecution on account of the word. In vv. 18f it is the turn of the seed which "fell among thorns" (4:7). Cares, delight, desire: for this third group the obstacles come from within man. Finally, v. 20, comes the turn of the seed which "fell into good soil" (4:8). These hear the word, accept it, and yield fruit.

1. Evaluation of the Explanation

Our evaluation of the Explanation of the Sower—whether it is more or less faithful to the parable—will, of course, vary according to our understanding of the parable. We may prefer to take the view that the Sower envisages the Kingdom triumphing over all difficulties, whereas the explanation has considered mainly the obstacles in the way of the fruition of the word or, perhaps more accurately, the failure of those who hear it. The parable is optimistic, full of hope, but the commentary is more aware of the difficulties and dangers and sounds a note of warning. However, it too closes on an encouraging note, for the hearers standing on the good ground hear, accept, and bear fruit. The explanation of the Sower looks to the individual and is, indeed, a psychological study. Every man who has heard the Gospel message is challenged to examine himelf seriously and to weigh up his reactions; for the word will find obstacles both outside of a man and within himself.

Again, we may take the Explanation in a somewhat different way. The seed is the Gospel preaching; this word is sown in the hearers, it is "seeded" in them (4:15). Four categories of hearers are distinguished in terms of the place where the seed has fallen: "along the path," "upon rocky ground," "among thorns," and "upon the good soil."

The fate of the word is different in each case. Satan comes and snatches the word as it is preached (v. 15). Initial joy at the hearing of the word will not compensate for lack of root. These are men of the moment who will not persevere in the face of tribulations and persecution. The description of the third category is the psychological analysis of a moralist who leans in great part on the explicit teaching of Jesus; much of it is redolent of the Sermon on the Mount. The fourth category is marked only by the manner in which these hearers receive the word: it is enough to be good soil, to be receptive, in order to bring forth fruit. This application is not unfaithful to the parable, once it is seen for what it is; for it only takes the subjective aspect of the proclamation and applies it to the hearers. They are shown that the story of the Sower does concern them. They are expected to be receptive to the proclaimed word of God. In his presentation of the traditional "interpretation" of the parable, Mark, less personal than Luke and Matthew, has emphasized the catechetical aspect of it. This catechesis, however, reset solidly on the basis of the revelation brought by Jesus.[2]

2. *The* Sitz im Leben *of the Explanation*

The Explanation is a product of the early Church. It came about because the Christians discovered to their shock and sorrow the truth that few really believed Jesus' message. They asked the burning question: how could it be that there was such a gulf between them and those who could not see? They found an answer in the words of the parable.

"Do not be dismayed by this experience. How could you expect it to be otherwise? Think what happens when the sower scatters his seed. Not every seed bears fruit. Much is lost for one reason or another." This understanding then led the first Christians to delineate the various oppositions to the Word which they saw happening around them in terms of the fourfold description they already had at hand in the parable. Thus, many men seem like the seed on the path: the word cannot reach them, as if the devil swiped it away at the very moment of receiving. Or, many men seem like shallow luxuriant growth: they are ready enough to receive, but they cannot persist. They have not had to face resistance, and so are not equal to resistance. Or, many men are like seed under thorns: they hear—but the word loses its significance because they are choked up by cares and distractions. The major concern of the Explanation is the structure of human life itself. The shallow mind, the hard heart, the preoccupations of the world, persecution—all these are precisely the obstacles which could frustrate the growth of faith. The Explanation assumes a period when christian belief was tested by cares, the deceit of riches, and persecution. It offers a warning and an encouragement to Christians in such conditions.

3. *The Message of Parable and Explanation*

To comment on the parable of the Sower is not the simple task it seems at first sight. Even when one tries to see it as something quite straightforward in Jesus' intention, one finds oneself influenced by the Explanation of the Sower which cannot help coloring the original parable. Most interpreters see the Sower as a parable of *contrast*. However, their differing viewpoints emerge in efforts to define exactly what this contrast consists of and where the emphasis in the parable lies. Some feel that it concerns the *growth* of the seed here and now in respect to the different soils. Others would place the emphasis on the *harvest*—an eschatological perspective in which the Sower with his seed meet the eschatological people of God and form a new creation. Again, the broader, and perhaps more vague, approaches would indicate a way in between the two and make use of both of them. This way would be to emphasize the importance of 'hearing' the eschatological word here and now.

There is a parallel variety of approach to the Explanation of the Sower. A whole gamut of comments have been applied to it, each one with some value. Whereas the parable was optimistic, the interpretation sounds a warning note. It has transferred the eschatological perspective to the psychological; it has given to the original parable an allegorization of every detail which it did not have. On the other hand, some have given a refreshingly new look to the Explanation from a positive viewpoint, giving it a fair trial. They feel that it, too, has a message and a promise: it too contains the great wonder that fruit is actually borne by some despite all the obstacles which we are only too well aware of without and within.

Somehow, far more important than the fine points of interpretation in both the Sower and its Explanation is the obvious general trend of the message they convey. Jesus is bolstering up confidence, quickening the faith of the *oligoi pistoi,* those of little faith. They had been plunged into doubt because of the apparent inefficacy of his ministry. He is assuring them: "Be of good heart. I have overcome the world" (Jn 16:33). He is summoning them to believe—and not only to believe but to actually trust in the ongoing of his Word despite the many who will not be able to receive it. The fact that some do receive and bear fruit is a marvellous sign of hope. God's purpose for his people is never defeated; it was so throughout salvation history, it was so for his Son, and it is so for us. This is the meaning of the Sower. The Explanation but shows us how, despite our dependence on him, God does demand our help. Are we soil such as can bear fruit? The answer is that we must turn to the message of the Sower again and hear Jesus' word aright: "He who abides in me and I in him, he it is that bears much fruit, for apart from me you can do nohing" (Jn 15:5).

(1) W. Neil, "The Sower (Mk 4:3-8)," *Expository Times* 77 (1965-66), 77.
(2) X. Leon-Dufour, *Études d'Evangile* (Paris: Seuil 1965), 288-292.

THE TREASURE
AND THE PEARL

The Parables, Mt 13:44-46

44. "The kingdom of heaven is like treasure hidden in a field, which a man found and covered up; then in his joy he goes and sells all that he has and buys that field.
45. Again, the kingdom of heaven is like a merchant in search of fine pearls, 46. who, on finding one pearl of great value, went and sold all that he had and bought it."

In Mt 13:44 we have a picture of what, to an outsider, must have seemed a bizarre transaction: a poor man who actually sells all he has in his poverty to buy a patch of ground! But, as we shall see, the point of both parables is that the finders are very willing to pay, without reserve, their prices, because they *know* the priceless nature of that which is, for each of them, the chance of a lifetime. The man had found "a hidden treasure": here we have a favorite theme in oriental folklore. Jesus must have been thinking of a jar containing silver coins or jewels—one of the small hoards which may still be uncovered today in Palestine during archaeological excavation or by chance. In the ancient world where there was much danger from brigandry and constant danger of foreign attack, the householder would bury his little store for safekeeping in a field, hoping one day to return and claim it. Jesus' listeners may have associated his words with a rabbinical parable about a poor scribe whose ox sinks into a hole while ploughing and breaks its leg. On going to help it out, the scribe discovers that the hole contains a treasure. In our parable, the man (who is so poor that he has to work someone else's land) "covered up" his treasure; he hid it again so that he can acquire the treasure *with* the field. Some readers have been bothered by the 'ethics' of the parable in that the finder does not tell the owner of the field about the treasure. But this factor is part of the trappings of the story, and it is idle to evaluate the conduct of the finder on legal or moral grounds.[1] The point of comparison in both parables is that the finders *buy*. They do not make a sacrifice but pay a purchase price in full awareness of the value of what they shall acquire. The purchase provides a unique opportunity.

In 13:45, by contrast, we have a wholesale trader, a big businessman who is well-to-do. He is in a strange land, perhaps among pearl fishers, where he comes upon "an especially valuable pearl." For it he relinquishes whatever he may have had on his beasts of burden or in his ship. And even when he sells all in order to obtain it, he is not paying for its *real* value, but only the price at which the present owner is ready to sell. The merchant knows very well what he is about. It may be that, originally, this second parable was more like the first. In the Gnostic *Gospel of Thomas*, in what may be an earlier version of the parable, the merchant is not specifically in search of pearls, so his find is just as unexpected as that of the hidden treasure. But we are interested here only in Matthew's story.

The Art of the Parables

The exegesis of the parables, which points out the situation which Jesus envisaged, and relates it to themes in oriental folklore, is the best commentary on their art form. As far as the oriental folklore theme goes, the uniqueness of these parables lies in their unexpected departure from the usual. Jesus' listeners would expect the finder of the treasure, for instance, to build a palace, or the pearl to be the means of saving the merchant when he was attacked by brigands. Jesus surprises his listeners by treating his stories in such a way as to emphasize an unexpected variation on a well-known theme. It is part of the "sage management" that the finder does not remove the treasure but buries it again to acquire it with the field. Only thus can the point of comparison, the unique opportunity of the Kingdom, be brought out. It is also part of the stage management that the finders must sell all. It is the narrator who sets a limit to the wealth of the merchant, and lets the finder discover the treasure in another's patch of land, being so poor that the purchase of the field exhausts what little he has. The parables describe fortunate happenings which are not part of Everyday...yet, are born of everyday. The laborer and the merchant are to be congratulated.

117

PARABLES TOLD BY JESUS

The Point of the Parables.

It is unlikely that the point Jesus is making lies in the ideas of hiddenness, searching and finding. Instead, three basic emphases in the parables have been defined: that of the *joy* in finding, that of the *value* of the find, and that of the *cost* involved. The theme of joy is explicit in the treasure parable—"in his joy"—; it is implicit in the other: the merchant in search of fine pearls cannot but have rejoiced at finding an especially valuable pearl. It is the joy which seizes a man and possesses him so fully that all else seems valueless. No price is too great. The man who lays hold of what God has prepared for him and invests all in it without reflection or hesitation does so with joy. To see the Kingdom at work, to share in its creation, brings such happiness that all fears, sombreness and risks are defeated and illumined by sheer joy.

There is the theme of the *cost*. This cannot be equated simply with Jesus' call to "renounce all," for it has its manifest reward here and now in the cause of Jesus. It is far more of a purchase, made deliberately, than a sacrifice. It is, of course, the total commitment of a son of the Kingdom. He must give up all he has. It includes the idea of sacrifice involved in discipleship, as can be glimpsed in Lk 14:27 (the daily cross), 14:26 (hating one's life), 9:62 (hand to the plough). However, all such texts do not quite express the nature of our parables' "sacrifice": It is a *response*: the disciple responds to God's Kingdom by committing himself without reserve to God's

118

will. But he is not surrendering everything expecting no reward. Rather he is buying, paying a purchase price, knowing full well what a bargain he has found.

This leads to the emphasis upon the *value* of what is discovered. Those who make the purchase are sure of the value beforehand. There is a cause-effect relationship between "finding" (value) and "selling all" (total investment). One might note that the value does include the sheer splendor of the discovery; the response is not to a categorical demand or to a naked word. The Kingdom is wealth beyond any other. Do we perceive this supreme value enough to "buy" it at the cost of everything?

The Existential Application of the Parables

In these parables Jesus is appealing for a specific course of action here and now, for a definite resolve. His argument is cogent—seeing that the Kingdom is identified with himself. In effect, he is saying, "You agree that the Kingdom is the highest good. It is a wealth which demonetizes all currency. It is in your power to possess it here and not if, like the treasure finder and the merchant, you will throw caution to the winds. *Are* you willing to part with all to gain it? Are *you?*"

To attach oneself to Jesus is to become a son of the Kingdom, because Jesus himself is the Kingdom—the *autobasileia*, in Origen's word. If one takes the parables as illustrating different manners of "finding"—the unexpected nature of the discovery by the one and the long search leading to the other's find—it could be a way of expressing

119

PARABLES TOLD BY JESUS

Jesus' awareness that different people take different roads to God's Kingdom. Whereas other parables are addressed to or deal with a group, these two concern the individual person. They are an example of the zeal—yes, of the avarice —with which the believer should pursue the Kingdom at any price. A man is faced with a decision. Will he be cautious and play safe, or will he embark on a course of action which to outsiders seems highly risky?

Yes, the parables do speak of absolute risk. How can it be defined? Is it part of the cost of discipleship as other gospel passages teach? We may hope to find the key in our own actual circumstances—that is, when we ourselves are confronted with the possibility of risking everything. The "nearness of time" is just as real today as then (cf. 2 Cor 6:2: Now is the acceptable time ...). The place where we can count on God's nearness has been revealed to us. Jesus has told us that it lies in those who need God. God's coming, his nearness, was to be in the sick, the poor, the sinners. Jesus' words and actions may point the way to this time and place, but, we must find it ourselves in Jesus' name. The claim made to God's nearness demands that all things be risked. Faith in Jesus means holding fast to the promise of God's nearness. Jesus brings us to the point where we wait for God's coming; he opens our eyes so that we do not miss his nearness. The parables are meant to uproot a man from indolence and lead him to vigilance, taking into account the gravity of the situation. Each situation calls for a decision. Each moment holds a rich opportunity. One must make the most of what lies hidden in every occasion.

Preaching the Parables

A first point to be made in grasping and conveying the message of these two parables is that of the contrast between the behavior of the finders and what those outside, 'they,' would expect. Would "they" not think the peasant a fool to impoverish himself utterly by buying the field, or the merchant incredibly rash? So it may seem at first sight: to those who do not understand it would seem ridiculous, utter folly, that these two should invest all they have, without any reflection or hesitation. The parables, however, teach that what seems to the outsider to be unwise, crazy indeed, is in fact the most sensible, wisest thing to do.

The wisdom of their choice can be found in the supreme call to follow Jesus. "Follow me!": this call describes the quality of the life which is overpowered by the great *joy* of finding the Kingdom. To follow Jesus means that the Kingdom becomes life's whole aim, filling the heart with gladness and with the *love* of this Lord who became a servant. It is ultimately because of him that we arrive at one of the major themes of the parables in terms of their applied message: namely, that no price can be too great. When the Christian realizes that it is Jesus he follows —that is, when he realizes who this Jesus really is—then it is a matter of course that he will make an unreserved surrender for that which is most valuable. Like finding a treasure or a pearl, only infinitely more marvellous, he cannot but perceive that the only value in life is this Lord. Thus, the decisive thing is not *what* a man gives up for him but his *reason* for doing so. A man gladly gives all of which he is capable if he grasps the sheer worth of his discovery. True, what God asks of us in following Jesus may be tailored to our own human capacity to give. But always we are getting so much more than we actually "pay" for.

Another important point in the message of the parables is the finders' *certainty* about what they want to acquire and its worth. They are both men who experience the splendor of the discovery. Their zeal is so aroused that they are willing to pay any price for the Kingdom. The merchant invests all in what he knows will repay him; the laborer buys the field because of the treasure he has seen. That which draws them is like a seductive force. They must abandon themselves in faith to an opportunity granted them.

The element of surprise—the unexpected—is also present in the parables. They can speak to us really only when we ourselves have been confronted with the possibility of having to risk all. They call for a response which throws caution to the winds and answers Jesus' call: "Follow me!" This response must be inspired by that personal quality in Jesus which impels one to pay any price, as a matter of course, for following him. And one does not hesitate to take this risk once it is grasped that the Kingdom *is* present in the person of Jesus whom we are called to follow. For the Kingdom does not come with observation or exclamations of "Lo, here it is!" or "There!" No: behold, "the kingdom of God is in the midst of you" (Lk 17:21)-- because "the Word became flesh and has pitched his tent among us" (Jn 1:14).

(1) J.D.M. Derrett (*Law in the New Testament,* London 1970, pp, 1-16) argues, persuasively, that in rabbical law the owner of the field had no rights in the treasure; the finder was perfectly entitled morally and in law, to act as he did. Jesus' hearers would have had no ethical problem.

THE PRODIGAL SON

The Prodigal Son is a rare, singular piece, a pearl among the parables. It is a work of conscious artistry touched by the genius of its Author. In contrast to most of the other parables, it shows no trace of the early Church's hand. The power of this parable derives from its economy of words, its finesse, and its lack of allegory and idealization. It remains on the human-temporal level, yet all of it points to the nature of God: "I have sinned against *God* and against *you.*"

The Parable, Lk 15:11-32

11. And he said: "There was a man who had two sons; 12. and the younger of them said to his father, 'Father, give me the share of property that falls to me.' And he divided his living between them. 13. Not many days later, the younger son gathered all he had and took his journey into a far country, and there he squandered his property in loose living. 14. And when he had spent everything, a great famine arose in that country, and he began to be in want. 15. So he went and joined himself to one of the citizens of that country, who sent him into his fields to feed swine. 16. And he would gladly have fed on the pods that the swine ate; and no one gave him anything. 17. But when he came to himself he said, 'How many of my father's

125

hired servants have bread enough and to spare, but I perish here with hunger! 18. I will arise and go to my father, and I will say to him, "Father, I have sinned against heaven and before you; 19. I am no longer worthy to be called your son; trust me as one of your hired servants."' 20. And he arose and came to his father. But while he was yet at a distance, his father saw him and had compassion, and ran and embraced him and kissed him. 21. And the son said to him, 'Father, I have sinned against heaven and before you; I am no longer worthy to be called your son.' 22. But the father said to his servants, 'Bring quickly the best robe, and put it on him; and put a ring on his hand, and shoes on his feet; 25. and bring the fatted calf and kill it, and let us eat and make merry; 24. for this my son was dead, and is alive again; he was lost, and is found.' And they began to make merry.

25. Now his elder son was in the field; and as he came and drew near to the house, he heard music and dancing. 26. And he called one of the servants and asked what this meant. 27. And he said to him, 'Your brother has come, and your father has killed the fatted calf, because he has received him safe and sound.' 28. But he was angry and refused to go in. His father came out and entreated him, 29. but he answered his father, 'Lo, these many years I have served you, and I never disobeyed your command; yet you never gave me a kid, that I might make merry with my friends. 30. But when this son of yours came, who has devoured your living with harlots, you killed for him the fatted calf!' 31. And he said to him, 'Son, you are always with me, and all that is mine is yours. 32. It was fitting to make merry and be glad, for this your brother was dead, and is alive; he was lost and is found.'"

According to the Jewish law of the day, the share of

the younger of two sons would be a third of his father's property. The young man in this story wants not only his share but also the right to dispose of it. He turns his property into cash and seeks an independent life abroad (v. 13); he wants to make his fortune in the more favorable conditions which prevailed in the Diaspora. Thus, his fault does not lie in his actually leaving home (as a younger son he had little option), but in his foolhardy living abroad. It is noteworthy that the father allows him tó depart without giving him the customary "instructions" at such a moment (cf. Tb 4:3-21) or without a plea to return. It is part of his willingness to give the boy total freedom.

The foolish young man very soon ran through his money and found himself, in face of a famine, quite penniless. In v. 15 no greater degradation could be pictured: not only is the son reduced to the lowest grade of agricultural workers among the Gentiles but he is forced to be in contact with animals which his religion branded as unclean; this implies that he was forced to renounce his regular religious practices. In v. 16 we are to read: he would gladly have eaten the carob beans (the bitter pods of the carob tree) on which the pigs fed, but he was too disgusted to share the food of pigs. But nothing else was given him to eat, so he was forced to steal. We may note a relevant rabbinical saying: "When the Israelites are reduced to eating carob pods, they repent!"

The "recognition scene" (vv. 17-19) presents the son as capable of "coming to himself" while he engages in a monologue which leads him to his decision to return. He is drawn primarily by memory of the father, by the sense of contrast between now and before, hunger and well-being, a strange land and home. In this hour of greatest need the prodigal must think of his father. The laconic character of the statement, "he came to himself," should be retained. It is not a matter of repentance or conversion—terms too lofty to describe his disposition at this stage. Rather, it is a matter of surprise, a new dimension coming from beyond himself. He knows he has forfeited his rights; therefore, he makes a new proposition relying completely on the will of his father.

And now the father emerges from the shadows to take the center stage (vv. 20-24). He is characterized entirely by his "going out to meet." He *ran*—it would be considered most undignified for an elderly oriental to run; but this is an exceptional man who will not be hampered by convention. The kiss on the cheek is a sign of forgiveness. It comes before the son can even acknowledge his guilt. The wonder of this meeting is the surprise it held for the son. Too much had happened for him to dare to believe that his father might really listen to him. But his father cuts through all his preconceptions, runs from afar, and recognizes in his very return his repentance. The whole point lies in the father's initiative. It is his overwhelming, unexpected behavior. The son can still acknowledge his guilt but he will no longer dare to suggest that he be reckoned as a hired servant; a like suggestion would be an insult to such love. All the while the father's actions have spoken louder than any words and when he does speak it is to give orders to his servants: the garments, signet ring and shoes signify the prodigal's reinstatement as a son of the family. It is enough that the son has returned; the rest is taken care of by *love,* the father's love which had never rejected him. Then followed a joyous feast, with song and dance: "For this my son has come back to life; he was lost and is found."

This would appear to mark the end of the parable—but it is not ended, the elder son has his place in it. The parable is a diptych and the emphasis falls on the second part. It concerns the fault of the older brother even beyond that of the younger. What comes to light now is that the elder son's sense of justice vehemently protests at a love which seems to confound all sense of values. He is, not so much upset by the feast or the calf or the kid as by the behavior of the father: this inconceivable love. He does not address his father as "Father." He will not call the prodigal brother —he is "this son of yours"! But the father addresses him as *teknon,* "my dear child," and gently reminds him who it is that has come back: "This *your brother* was dead and is alive, he was lost and is found"—it was right that we should make merry and rejoice (v. 32). But all of this seems absurd, seems outrageous, to the elder son who cannot see what is motivating the father and how he can be so happy. That is, he does not understand the nature of love. It is he, and not the prodigal, who is in danger of becoming a "hired servant" (v. 19). Indeed, by his insistence on service and obedience (v. 29) he shows himself to have the mentality of a servant and not the conviction of being son.

The Setting

The setting of the parable is indicated in Lk 15:2: there the Pharisees and scribes murmur at Jesus' table-fellowship with sinners, and Jesus speaks this parable—along with the Lost Sheep and the Lost coin—as a vindication of his message. The "Lost Boy" is his defense of the Good News for the Poor[1] rather than an actual proclamation of it. Thus, he demonstrates that the Pharisees were wrong. But he does so quietly, in a spirit of love. He speaks of a parallel to the real situation. The younger son leads a life in conflict with the commands of God and serves the Gentiles; this makes him like the sinners and tax collectors with whom Jesus associated. The elder son has never transgressed a single command of the father; this is like the Pharisees' fidelity to the letter of the Law. Jesus does not condemn them, however, he rather pities their blindness and calls for love to meet love. He does not dispute with them; he reveals a God they do not really know. He speaks to them in parable and they are left to draw their own conclusion. He calls to cease from their loveless, joyless ways and to rejoice with the rising and the returning! His polemic is armed with gentle love.

The Art of the Parable

The Prodigal Son is not allegory; it is a story drawn from life, from our own pool of experience, and transformed by Jesus' vision. The characters have an existence in their own

130

right—as if their creator (Jesus) had liberated them from a historical situation and given them an existence in the universal consciousness of man. The characters are shown without comment by the Narrator—one could say that they are refreshingly free of exegesis! The parable's artistic quality is confirmed in the very begining when we read: "There was a man who had two sons." They remain anonymous—but immortal.[2] The persons achieve a typical existence and their actions present archetypal patterns of human behavior because the parable is a literary creation. It is this that gives it such scope for existential application. The first part of it depicts the journey of Everyman through departure, estrangement, longing, dissolution and final return born of anguish. The unexpected forgiveness experienced by the prodigal represents the manner in which "God always works all things for good" (Rm 8:28) in our own lives when we least anticipate it. It is that new dimension to life made possible through Jesus as Savior.

From a literary standpoint, the parable can be seen to progress in three stages: the son leaves home and drifts into degradation; the father sees the boy from afar; "now his elder son was in the field." This makes it a perfect short story in which the "sage management" has been artfully arranged. The father sees the son at a distance; this means that he must go out to meet him, running. The elder son does not come from the field until the feast is already underway: this allows his protest to be revealed in his very refusal to join in the feast. The father's generosity is demonstrated in his gesture of going out to meet both sons.

PARABLES TOLD BY JESUS

The father of the story is a veiled reference to God, and yet always an earthly father. He is presented exclusively as one who loves. In his goodness and grace, he rejoices over the return of the lost; the focus is on the "prodigal father," prodigal of love. His actions are surprising but not incredible; as such, they cut through the ordinary way of looking at things and point to God's ways. He takes a two-fold risk: that of increasing the profligacy of one son and arousing the anger of the others (both by his incredible generosity). As compared with the father in the parable of the Wicked Vinedressers (Lk 20:9-18), who is sovereign and conscious of his power, the father of the two sons, despite his estate, servants and manifest authority, is pictured only in terms of love and paternal indulgence. In using the "father image" Jesus is not contradicting the image of absolute Lord of the prophets. Paternity is founded on Lordship. And what seems to be weakness in the father's actions is really his strength.

The Homiletic Aspect

Jesus' purpose in the parable is to state the fundamental principle of God's dealing with sinners. The sinner is loved before he can repent; he is never cut off. And when he does repent, God restores him to his own family. Jesus says to his critics that he consorts with sinners precisely because God is a loving Father who welcomes the repentant sinner. He claims that in him God's love for the sinner is made actual; he is acting as God's representative. Everything hinges on the initiative of the father whose goodness spans

132

both halves of the parable. He acts as if nothing ever happened to come between him and his son. And the hour of their reunion is the hour of candor: the son must openly acknowledge his fault—not because this will win him another chance, but because nothing else is possible once he has realized his fault in the light of his father's love.

Yet, everything leads up to the final scene. The elder son is one who keeps himself at a distance, always cuts himself off. All depends on whether or not he will understand the language of love. Will the elder son, always at home, end up more distant from the father than the younger son who had returned from a distance? The elder son is thus *confronted* with his younger brother: will he, at last, recognize him as brother? The relationship determines that between him and the father: *only* by receiving his brother as brother can he truly know his father and know himself as son. If the elder could but find his way to the feast which the father has arrayed, he too would be filled with joy and would be united with his brother at the father's table.

The parable finds its relevance in the repeated themes of joy and love (rather than in any emphasis on the guilt of the prodigal). The father summons the elder brother to abandon his aloofnes and share the joy of his family table; he restores the younger to this joy as a free gift. Jesus is calling his hearers to this same fellowship of joy; he yearns for them to accept his welcoming invitation. And, as in the whole of Jesus' ministry, the great scandal—the offence—is his and his Father's love. The father in the parable is he who loves, who takes the initiative, who is prodigal of love. And can we not say that the prodigal too (in contrast to his brother) is one who knows the reality of love? He knew love's pain in remembering a father who had never cast him off; he trusted in that love ... and he returned.

Chapter VII.
(1) See W. Harrington, "The Mission of Jesus: Preaching Good News to the Poor," *The Furrow* 23 (1972), 511-525.
(2) "Nowhere in the world's literature has such immortality been conferred on anonymity," G.V. Jones, *The Art and Truth of the Parables* (London: S.P.C.K. 1964), 124.

Bibliography

C.H. Dodd, *The Parables of the Kingdom* (London: Collins 1961³).

J. Jeremias, *The Parables of Jesus* (London: SCM 1963²).

J.D.M. Derrett, *Law in the New Testament* (London: Darton, Longman & Todd 1970).

G. Eichholz, *Gleichnisse der Evangelien*. Form, Uberlieferung, Auslegung (Neukirchen-Vluyn: Neukirchener Verlag 1971).

G.V. Jones, *The Art and Truth of the Parables* (London: S.P.C.K. 1964).

H. Kahlefeld, *Parables et lecons dans l'Evangile*, 2 vols. Paris: Cerf 1969.

J.D. Kingsbury, *The Parables of Jesus in Matthew 13* (London: S.P.C.K. 1969).

E. Linnemann, *Parables of Jesus*. Introduction and Exposition (London: S.P.C.K. 1969).

D.O. Via, *The Parables*. Their Literary and Existentialist Dimension (Philadelphia: Fortress Press 1967).

A. Weiser, *Die Knechtsgleichnisse der Synoptischen Evangelien* (München: Kösel-Verlag 1971).